2

FABRIC
Painting

FABRIC Painting

MARY ELIZABETH RATCLIFFE

PHOTOGRAPHY BY JOHN COOK

a Salamander book

Published by Salamander Books Limited
LONDON • NEW YORK

A SALAMANDER BOOK

Published by Salamander Books Ltd,
52 Bedford Row,
London WC1R 4LR,
United Kingdom.

© Salamander Books Ltd 1988

ISBN 0 86101 373 5

Distributed in the UK by
Hodder & Stoughton Services,
PO Box 6,
Mill Road,
Dunton Green,
Sevenoaks,
Kent TN3 2XX.

All correspondence concerning the contents of this volume should
be addressed to Salamander Books Ltd.

CREDITS
EDITOR: CHARLOTTE MORTENSSON
ART DIRECTOR: BOB GORDON
STYLING: CHARLOTTE MORTENSSON
ILLUSTRATIONS: SANDRA POND
TYPESETTING: H&P GRAPHICS LTD, ENGLAND
COLOUR REPRODUCTION: YORK HOUSE GRAPHICS LTD, ENGLAND
PRINTED IN ITALY

CONTENTS

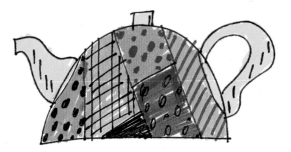

PREFACE

Designing textiles has, over the years, brought me tremendous joy, pleasure and satisfaction. Finding the time to do this has not always been easy—leading a busy life, lecturing at Art Schools, as well as running a home with my husband and two teenage sons, has meant that there have often been conflicting demands on my time. However, it has always been extremely important for me to continue creating and designing, and my family have become used to my obsession with fabrics. They have also accepted my ever-growing collection of strange paraphernalia — china, costumes, jewellery, fabrics and old illustrated books — which I have collected from markets and antique shops over the years to give me inspiration for my work.

In this book I have tried to convey the pleasure I have found in working with textiles and colour. Everyone possesses the ability to be creative with pattern and colour. We all respond differently to stimuli, and it is this personal interpretation and application that ensures so much wonderful variety in art and design.

In addition to a willingness to experiment and try new ideas, a degree of practical knowledge is essential for fabric painting and printing. I have introduced the reader to different fabric painting techniques and methods of working. Through my job as a textiles lecturer, I understand the problems involved in tackling designs and their practical application. I hope that this book, with its step-by-step instructions will give the reader the practical knowledge and the confidence to try things themselves. The amount of time spent working on each project will vary according to each individual's way of working, but the most important thing is to have fun.

It is always a great thrill for me to see my designs on a fabric roll in a shop or worn by people in the street. So too, will seeing your fabrics being used around the home give a tremendous sense of pleasure and achievement. I trust that, through this book, many more people will learn to express themselves through fabric design. Do not be intimidated—everyone can make something original.

Mary Elizabeth Ratcliffe

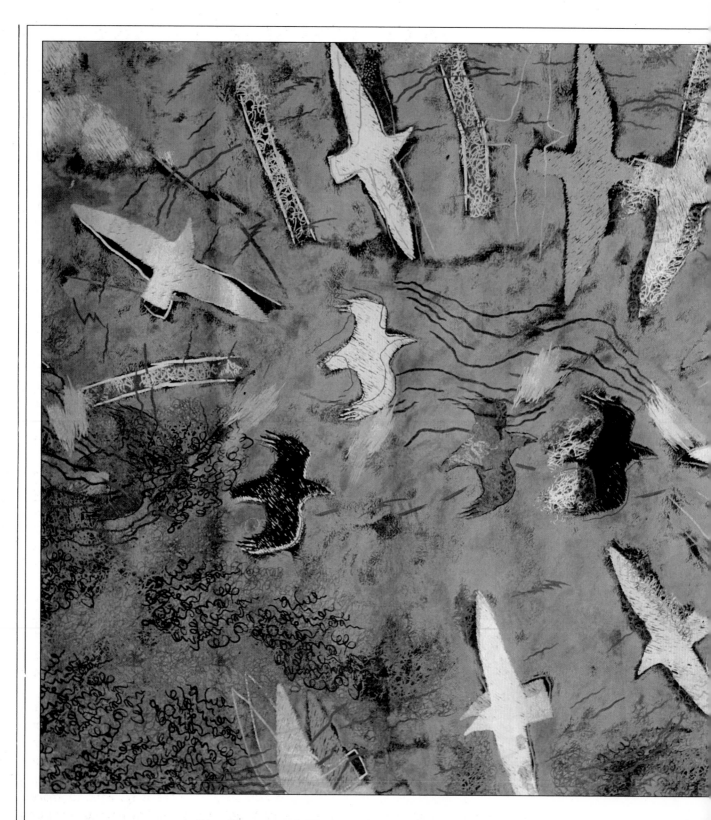

This wall hanging, entitled 'Fulmar and Crows', is by Nicola Henley.
It combines the easily recognizable shapes of birds in flight with more
contemporary textures, using rich colours with gold and black for dramatic effect.

INTRODUCTION

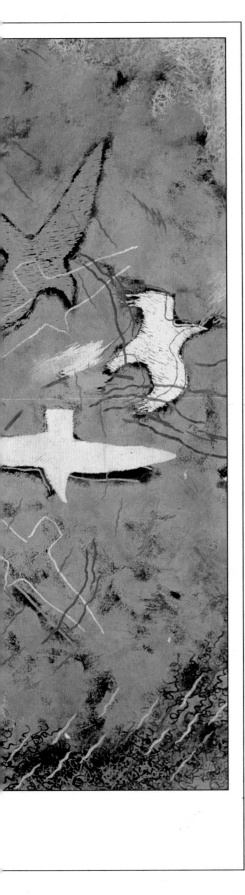

Despite the vast array of fabrics available in our shops, it can still be very difficult to find the design or the colour that we are looking for to co-ordinate with our decorative ideas. Certainly, there is a tremendous selection to choose from—from traditional and ornate to modern and abstract. However, few of these will appeal to the discerning shopper who is looking for a fabric that has something unusual and exciting to offer.

The solution, which is also a very enjoyable one, is to design and decorate your own fabrics. This book aims to assist you in developing and executing your own ideas onto fabrics, producing interesting and exciting things for your own home.

For most of us, our home environment is tremendously important, and a great deal of thought, time and money is invested in enhancing and developing the character of our house or flat. In creating the mood for our homes, the use of fabric is probably the most important factor. Whatever the size of the bedroom, kitchen, living room or bathroom, an imaginative use of pattern and decoration will introduce an exciting element to the decor, reflecting the owner's personality, interests and taste.

This is certainly not a new concept. During the 1920s, there was a noticeable lessening of the differences between dress and furnishing fabrics. This revolution was due mainly to the influence of Paul Poiret, who was probably the first couturier to combine the designing of women's clothes with interior decoration. His work expressed a harmony of design which indiscriminately used printed fabrics for dress fabrics and furnishings.

Trends in fashion have continued to influence interior design, and the broad range of styles now available in clothes is increasing our awareness of the design potential of our homes. As in fashion, individual and unusual combinations of fabric can create a strong, interesting effect, which can range from bold and striking to soft and romantic, depending upon the mood we want to create.

Fashions come and go, and we could not possibly afford to change our room interiors at the same rate that we discard and replace our clothes. The life span of a room setting, using durable modern materials, makes it impractical and uneconomical to consider major changes every season. However, adding your own fabrics to a room can radically alter its mood and atmosphere. There is no need to make expensive or permanent commitments. Simply adding new cushions or a wall hanging in your living room can alter the whole character of the room. Changes can be dramatic, or can gently blend into the decor, subtly adding interest to your home.

LEARNING ABOUT COLOUR AND DESIGN

Colour is the prime factor of any design scheme and its importance cannot be over-emphasized. There are no longer any strict rules governing the use of colour and its combinations. Interior designers were often the victims of colour clichés—for instance, a scarlet room would be considered to be stimulating and exciting, an orange room was thought to make the inhabitant forceful and aggressive, a yellow room was delightfully luminous, a green room still and placid, blue was quiet and spiritual, white unemotional, grey, neutral. These ideas are still in force to some extent today, but the use of colour is much more flexible and colours are selected according to personal likes and dislikes, rather than by rules and regulations.

It is, therefore, important to learn about colour—to find out how it can be used and which colours we find appealing. An enjoyable and rewarding way of discovering colour and its application is by studying the work of artists and designers. A visit to an art gallery will give you the opportunity to do this and to discover how you respond to various approaches to paints, drawings, etchings etc. Over the years, designers have looked to artists for inspiration, and a number of artists have produced textile designs. The most notable of these artists were Matisse, Delaunay and Dufy, all of whom saw the potential for expression through this decorative medium.

During my own many visits to art galleries, there have been some notable occasions when the quality of colour and the use and application of paint have greatly affected my understanding of colour and have been a useful source of ideas for design work. The first time was seeing an exhibition of Mark Rothko's work at the Tate Gallery in London. The rich warmth created by the use of a strictly limited range of colour was very profound. The intense impact of his use of colour—red on an orange background, or blue on another shade of blue—can be very simply adapted to fabric painting by applying dyes to a strong, heavyweight canvas. The colours can be sponged onto the fabric to build up a rich vibrant effect.

Monet's paintings of waterlilies also greatly inspired me because of the quality of colour and his use of many hues of blue, lilac and green. The impact of Monet's work, and indeed, that of other impressionist painters, can be adapted by the fabric painter to create a large wall hanging on a cotton or linen fabric. Monet had drawn his inspiration from the waterlilies in his orangerie, but the subject you choose could capture the intensity of the colour without being limited to detailed forms. The quality of colour can be achieved by applying the dye very thickly onto the cotton or linen, using a variety of utensils. Brushes of different sizes can be dragged and dabbed onto the cloth, creating layers of colour, varying in tone and quality. Scrunched rags, dipped into dye can be pressed against the cloth, leaving areas of pure colour.

Another early experience, which taught me a great deal about colour, particularly the use of gold, was a visit to Ravenna in Italy, where I saw the fabulous coloured mosaics. Many of the mosaics incorporated gold,

Robert and Sonia Delaunay both worked to develop and portray colour in their paintings. This painting called 'Windows Open Simultaneously' is by Robert. It shows the beautiful quality of colour, using complementary and contrasting shades. The simple shapes are placed against each other, enhancing the sophisticated colourings.

It was Sonia Delaunay who saw the potential in designing for textiles and costumes. Her exquisite understanding of colour achieved effects which were innovative and lovely, although the designs for fashion did little to complement the figure!

which, when combined with turquoise and orange, produced a breath-taking, rich effect. Gold dyes are available from art shops, but they are expensive. However, if a full, golden effect is desired, the outlay is worthwhile. Alternatively, gold can be mixed by blending yellow and black and adding a little red.

Mosaics are made up of small coloured pieces of glass and stone, and this technique can be adapted to fabric. By cutting a number of square wooden blocks or, more simply, cutting a square shape out of a potato, the blocks or potatoes can be dipped into a dye, and an image built up from the squares. Imperfections will occur in the printing, which will add variety to the square form, rather like the variety of cut shapes or broken squares seen in mosaics.

Design and colour influences can be pictorial or purely abstract. An example of how an artist can influence the work of textile designers is Jackson Pollock. His splashed and dripped paintings have been copied and reproduced by both fashion and interior designers. Jackson Pollock's ideas can easily be interpreted by splashing colours directly on to cloth, producing exciting, stimulating effects.

There is also a wealth of ideas and inspiration to be gleaned from the work of a variety of decorative artists such as jewellers, potters and sculpturers. Remember, too, that the work of craftsmen stretches back over many centuries and encompasses every part of the world.

LEFT: 'The Snail', painted by Matisse, has a timeless quality and a beauty which remains inspirational to this day. The simple use of shapes placed against each other gives a marvellous effect. Not only has the positioning of the coloured shapes been given careful consideration, but the background forms left by the coloured shapes play a strong part in this work too.

By using one or more simple shapes in your own work, a strong design effect can be achieved. The idea is not to copy Matisse, but to enjoy his work and to develop your own sense of placing and building shapes.

RIGHT: The characteristic paint effects used by Jackson Pollock have been used many times by both fashion and furnishing designers. The simple splashed and dripped images can be used to create lively and impressive effects which can easily be executed by even very inexperienced fabric decorators.

FINDING INSPIRATION

It is not, of course, possible for everyone to visit art galleries and museums. Fortunately, we can learn about design and about shape from an infinite number of sources. If you live in the country, a flower, an insect, a sunset or a leaf could inspire you and form the basis of a motif. Designs based upon natural forms are often rounded and free-flowing. For city dwellers, studying buildings, tiles and bricks may lead you towards more geometric work, using basic shapes. Brightly coloured shops, decorative, historical architecture or the shapes of rooftops from an upstairs window may lead you down other exploratory avenues. Alternatively, the sea, rivers, the zoo, a children's playground, are all potential sources of imagery.

Always carry a camera or a sketchbook with you to record images which you may later want to develop in your fabric design work. Not only will the sketches or photographs serve as a memory aid, physically recording the image will develop your 'eye', forcing you to become more aware of imagery and composition.

Many artists prefer to work purely from their own imaginations developing very personal themes. If you decide to work in this way, it will probably involve a considerable amount of time spent with pens and paper formulating your ideas.

Another approach to fabric painting is spontaneous design, using

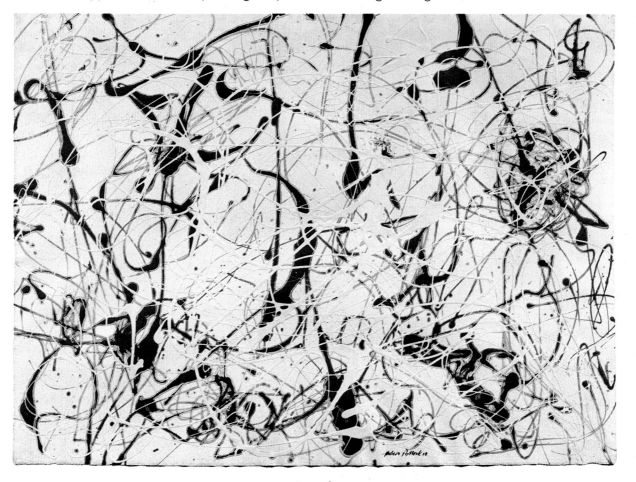

objects that you find appealing such as fruits, kitchen utensils, pieces of children's toys, stones or shells. Such objects can be dipped into the paint and pressed onto the cloth in a free arrangement. However, this technique is often more successful, particularly for the beginner, if the arrangement of the motifs is planned beforehand.

Remember that elaborate designs do not necessarily mean a successful result. Beautiful images can be created by using only black and white or a primary colour in a very simple pattern. For instance, a bedcover which has been spattered with just one or two bright colours, or which has a very simple motif stencilled around the borders, can become a stunning centrepiece in the bedroom.

It can be difficult to envisage how a fabric design or particular project will be successful in your home. You may want to sketch the room, with the project you are designing—a rug, or curtains perhaps—in situ. Obviously, you will have to adhere firmly to the actual colours of the room and the ones that you are planning to use to get an accurate impression of the effect that you will achieve. If you find it difficult to sketch, a camera can be used. Take photographs of the room and the areas of it to which you plan to introduce textiles. Photocopies should then be taken of the photographs. Now try out different designs and colours on the images of your room by adding shapes and colours quite freely, creating a collage effect.

RIGHT: This lovely example of fabric painting is immediately recognizable as a print by William Morris (1834-1896), who founded the Arts and Crafts movement in England. William Morris possessed a deep understanding of nature and his designs were always based on flowers, birds, trees, plants, insects and animals. His work clearly illustrates his love of nature and colour, and was the forerunner of the Omega workshops, where people sought to decorate their homes with beautiful fabrics designed to express an enjoyment of pattern and colour.

LEFT: The stunning beauty of the mosaics at Ravenna were created by building up the images with small pieces of coloured stone. The sampler (above) shows how the technique can be interpreted for fabric design by block printing onto fabric. By using small cut squares, a pattern can be built up which, when viewed from a distance, conveys the overall image of the pattern. The irregularities of the block printing give a similar effect to the broken misshapen stone pieces of the mosaics.

RIGHT: 'The Harvest', by Raoul Dufy, has a wonderful decorative quality achieved by lovely use of colour and fluid marks. Little attention has been given to detail—the impact of the picture is as an impression of a scene. This is a style which can so easily be adapted for textile design by applying colour to the fabric and then painting or drawing over the material with darker fabric crayons or paints.

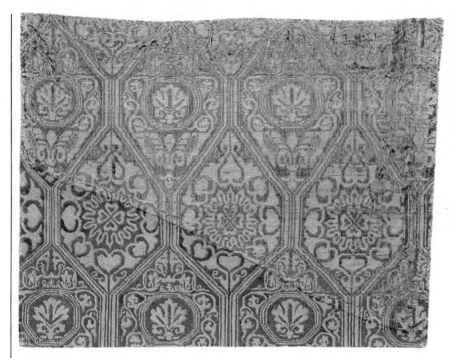

LEFT: Executed on silk twill tissue, this Byzantine fabric dates back to the late part of the 11th century. Despite the fact that only two colours are used, the regular, well-organized pattern achieves considerable richness. To achieve a similar design, fabric could be dyed to the desired background colour and printed with a darker colour for the design.

UNDERSTANDING FABRICS

It is not always necessary to use expensive fabrics for your work, particularly when you are trying out new techniques. If the fabric is relatively inexpensive, you will be able to be more experimental, and mistakes will not seem too disastrous. Decide how the fabric is going to be used and consider the qualities of a variety of materials before making a decision. The way in which fabric is draped or hung can achieve very different effects, depending upon the type of material used. Silk has a unique, shimmering quality, wools give a great depth of colour and cotton and linen have strong, earthy qualities. Bear in mind, too, the texture of the surface of the fabric, which will affect the printing.

You do not have to restrict yourself to working on white fabrics. As long as the manufacturer's finish is removed, dyeing is possible. Some experiments with different background colours and fabric paints will be necessary to learn how the colours of the paints are affected by the background cloth. Some printing colours are transparent and will not show up on dark background colours. If a very strong background colour is selected, all printing colours will be affected by it. For example, a bright red cotton fabric will not allow you to achieve a clean yellow or a lime green tone. In this case, better results would be achieved by printing darker tones, such as brown or black onto the red. Even then, the quality of colour might be slightly altered.

Interesting effects can also be achieved by working on patterned fabrics, for instance spots or checks. A checked fabric can be very useful if your design is based upon a grid formation.

When buying fabric, it is advisable to buy a little more than you need to give you the option of preparing test strips to see the effect of your chosen colours on the correct fabric.

ABOVE: This bold French design relies on simple shapes and the effective use of colour which lends itself to free interpretations. Note the black and white checked areas which are regularly placed over the design to create areas of contrast.

UNDERSTANDING PAINTS

It is not necessary to buy a vast number of colours for fabric painting. A small selection of primary colours will give you an ample choice from which to mix a large range of colours. Yellow, red, blue, black and white will give you enough versatility to blend a full range of colours. For instance, yellow and red will make orange; yellow and blue will make green; yellow and black will make a dull green; red and black will make brown.

Darker shades can be achieved by adding black or blue, and lighter shades can be achieved by adding white. If you are mixing pastel shades, it is always a good idea to add the colour to white, and not the other way around.

The above information is only given as a general guideline. Colour is a very personal thing, and its perception depends entirely upon personal taste and appreciation.

It should be remembered that paint will react differently on different types of fabric. A red will look strong on a heavyweight cotton, but the same colour, when used on a fine fabric, will appear much paler because of the transparent quality of the fabric and because the paint will tend to bleed into the fabric.

Once you have gathered together your design ideas and decided what you want to produce for your home, you will want to start investigating the various ways and techniques which can be used to transfer your ideas onto fabric.

Above: The simplicity of the shapes and figures depicted on this hand-painted Egyptian funeral cloth, hold an immense appeal and fascination up to this day. This beautiful example of early textile decoration can teach today's fabric designer a great deal about the value of clean, clear lines. The wonderful aged quality of the finely woven linen can be recreated today by experimenting with different fabric dyes and crayons.

Above Left: The visual impact of this 18th century Turkish cloth is created by the positioning of the patterns around the border. The use of regularly positioned patterns around the outer edge of a fabric can be adapted for tablecloth designs.

FABRIC PAINTING TECHNIQUES

When using any of the techniques listed below, the advice given in 'Before You Start' (page 24) must be followed.

Brush Strokes

This method is probably the simplest of all fabric painting techniques. It allows you total freedom to make direct marks and strokes onto the fabric. The range of brush marks can be as varied as your use of brushes. Large household brushes, scrubbing brushes, decorator's paint brushes and the finest sable brushes can all be used. Experiment with shapes, equipment and colour to develop imaginative new techniques and methods as you progress.

Once you have created a pleasing design, it should be transferred onto fabric in the following way. Keeping the sketch near at hand, use a light pencil to draw the design on the fabric. Once washed, the pencil marks will disappear. Begin by painting the lightest colour on the fabric and work through to the darker shades. Each colour should be allowed to dry thoroughly before applying the next shade. It is best to work from top to bottom to avoid smudging the paint. Always follow the manufacturer's instructions given for painting and for making the design permanent. Unless otherwise stated, most fabric paints are made permanent by ironing.

Spattering and Splashing

This lively technique is great fun because it can be successfully tackled by anyone, whatever their technical abilities. Colours are simply flicked onto fabric using a toothbrush, household brush or a stick, depending upon the effect that is desired. The splash effect is achieved by dipping the brush or stick into the paint and flicking the paint onto the fabric by jerking the wrist downwards. A stronger effect will be achieved by moving the arm from the elbow. You will be surprised at the variety of effects which be be achieved by using different arm movements. The size of the brush will also, of course, determine how wide the splash marks of paint are.

If possible, this technique should be employed outside, where it will not matter about stray blobs of paint. If you are working inside, cover all surfaces of the room with layers of newspaper, old sheets or plastic sheeting. Stray blobs of paint will be difficult to remove.

Sponging

This is also a very simple technique, requiring little skill or experience. A natural sponge or crumpled up balls of rag or newspaper are dipped into fabric paint and pressed onto the material, forming textured areas of colour. It is important that you do not overload the sponge or rags with paint or the textured effect will be lost. Apply the lightest colour first. It is not always necessary to allow each colour to dry before applying the next, as the blending of colours can produce lovely shades and tones.

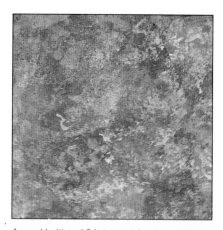

ABOVE: Undiluted fabric paint has been dabbed onto fabric using a coarse household brush. Note the areas of glitter paint used to highlight the rich, autumnal colours of the fabric.

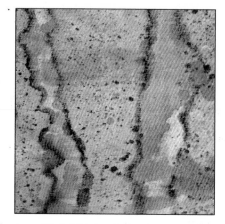

ABOVE: Diluted fabric paint has been sponged over cotton to create loose bands of colour which have freely bled into the material. Paint has then been spattered over the fabric.

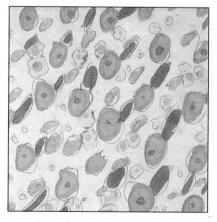

ABOVE: Blobs of silk paint have been carefully sponged on to fine silk and then encircled with a fabric pen, creating a fresh, flowery image.

Tie Dyeing

This is probably one of the oldest methods of fabric decoration. Again, it is fairly simple, requiring a neat, methodical approach to the work, rather than great artistic flair. The equipment needed is simple and inexpensive—the fabric to dye, a ball of string and a bowl of dye. The fabric is either knotted or tied tightly with string, so that when it is submerged in the dye bath, the colour cannot penetrate the areas which have been tightly tied up. Once the dye process is complete, and the fabric is opened out, a streaky pattern of undyed material will be left on a coloured background.

Thin fabrics, such as muslin or silk, take dye easily, whereas heavier fabrics will have to be submerged for a longer time in the dye bath. Any make of dye can be used, but if you are colouring a synthetic material, it is essential to use a dye recommended for man-made materials.

The dye process can be repeated many times over to create a variety of lovely colour patterns on the fabric. Remember that dye is transparent, so it is important to dye a fabric to a darker colour than its original colour.

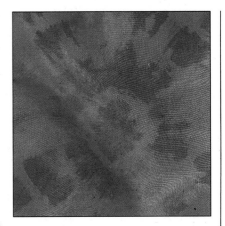

ABOVE: This fabric has been knotted and immersed in a dye bath to create a traditional tie dyed pattern.

Micro Dyeing

This is a new technique which is based on the traditional tie dyeing technique. The item to be dyed is tied, pleated or knotted and immersed in a dye bath which is placed inside a microwave oven for four minutes. This method is just as effective as the traditional technique and is, of course, much quicker. However, the size of the items which can be dyed is determined by the size of your microwave. Larger items, such as bedspreads, sheets, etc. are out of the question!

Batik

This is the Javanese name for a very ancient method of fabric design. The pattern on the material is made by painting a design onto the fabric with hot wax before immersing it in a dye bath. The wax prevents the dye reaching the painted areas and the finished cloth shows the pattern created by the wax on a coloured background. The dried wax can be deliberately cracked to form lines of colour where the dye can penetrate the fabric. The dye bath must be cold, as the wax will be removed by heat. Thin, smooth fabrics are the easiest to work on when using this technique, particularly if you are preparing a delicate pattern.

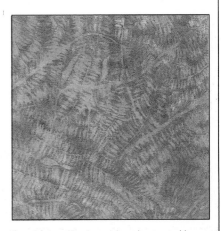

Stencilling

Stencilling is the process of spraying or painting colour through a cut piece of paper or cardboard onto fabric to create a clean-edged motif which can be repeated again and again. Simple shapes are often the most successful. Oiled stencil card which will not tear easily can be bought from art shops. However, acetate is preferred by many people because it is transparent, making it easy to trace designs onto it. By varying the position of the stencil on the fabric, a pattern can be built up using a variety of colours and shapes.

ABOVE: Interesting images can be created by using leaves or flowers as stencils, spraying fabric paint around the leaves.

Block Printing

A block is cut so that the pattern to be printed is in relief. This means that every part of the pattern which should not be transferred on to the fabric must be cut away. Blocks can be made from a large variety of objects, each with different characteristics. A potato block can be made by cutting a potato in half and printing small, repeating patterns on to the fabric.

Potatoes can be used very successfully on smooth materials such as silk and untextured cotton. They are not hard enough to be pressed on with a lot of pressure, so should not be used on heavy, coarse materials.

Rubber and cork can be cut into various shapes and sizes. The material to be printed must be pinned on to the working surface very tautly. Again, the best results will be achieved on a fine material.

Printing blocks made of lino are very successful, but special lino cutting tools must be purchased to gouge the pattern out of the lino. The block should be slightly larger than the design, and the image is traced on to it using carbon paper. Once cut, the block is most successfully used on smooth fabrics. Rougher materials can be used for all types of block printing, but the uneven quality of the fabric will give a print which is less clear. However, a textured effect can often be successfully incorporated into the design.

Lino printing is particularly lovely when transferred on to a fine chiffon, but the quantity of dye used for the pattern must be limited, or a stiffening effect will spoil the lightness and delicacy of the fabric.

Screen Printing

Screen printing is used commercially for printing most types of fabrics. It is really a refined variation of stencilling. Commercial screen printing techniques are very sophisticated and could not possibly be considered for home use. The screen printing process involves forcing ink across a cut stencil on to the fabric that you are printing. The stencil has been positioned inside a rectangular wooden frame which is then placed over the fabric.

A simple frame can be made at home by stretching organdie or a special screen mesh, which can be bought from most art shops, over an old picture frame. Alternatively, an inexpensive frame can be bought. The design is traced onto the organdie, and the areas not to be printed are blocked out with varnish. Alternatively, a paper stencil is cut and placed on the screen. The areas of the stencil which have been cut away will allow the colour to pass through to form the shape of the design.

Screen printing allows an pattern to be accurately repeated on a fabric, giving clean, clear edges to the work. However, it does require more time and dedication than most of the other techniques discussed in this book.

There are many variations possible to the above techniques, such as transfer painting, printing with fruit and vegetables, rope printing, etc. Fabric can also be decorated with a combination of techniques such as hand-painting and block printing, or sponging combined with spattering.

ABOVE: This fabric has been photographically screen printed, giving clear definition of colour and shape. With practice, the same definition of line can be achieved when printing by hand.

There really are no limits to the ideas that can be developed and the enjoyment that can be found in exploring different techniques and colours to produce original images. However, before you tackle a large project such as a bedcover or curtains, it is a good idea to try out your ideas on smaller items such as napkins or cushion covers. These pieces will be less demanding and mistakes will not matter so much if only a small amount of fabric and dyes have been wasted.

Mistakes can sometimes be rectified by making the printed colour permanent by ironing and then over-dyeing the cloth in a dye bath. This will achieve a more harmonious colour effect. Accidental blotches or splashes of colour can sometimes be disguised by stencilling over them with a new shape or by incorporating them into a hand-painted design. An exciting way to utilize a disappointing fabric is to cut or tear it into strips of cloth which are then reassembled by weaving or sewing them together. Some of the strips of fabric can be reversed or even removed altogether.

DEVELOPING YOUR IDEAS

Being imaginative with colours, textures and patterns will produce interesting textile work. The creative process need not stop after the design application has been completed. The use of traditional needle-work techniques such as patchwork, quilting or embroidery can further enhance your work. Again there are no rules to adhere to because any construction or piecing together of fabrics is viable. Your own personal ideas can be tried out, using mixed patterns and colours. Contrasting threads and wools can be embroidered on to your work to give it an exciting new dimension, or shapes can simply be glued on to the material. Working on fabric which has been cut into a specific shape, rather than printing on a continuous length of fabric is always interest-ing and challenging. However, discipline will be necessary when consi-dering the space allocated to the decorative work, as its proportion and scale are important.

No book about design would be complete without some mention of the advances made in computer aided design. This method of design can be tremendous fun to use. It is very quickly understood, and little time or experience is needed before the user can be creative and imaginative. A variety of lines, textures and colours can be used to play around with, giving a lively range of different effects. It is, however, difficult to reproduce the precise quality of colour that is seen on the screen. Possibly the best paint medium to do this in is transfer inks, which have a special luminosity and brightness.

It has been said that nothing in this world is original, it has all been done before. However, this jaded cliché is obviously not true. It is you who makes your work original, through your own personal style and interpretation, whether you are adapting an old design, or freely painting from a beautiful vase of flowers. However you choose to approach fabric painting and design, you will find that it is an exciting and rewarding experience.

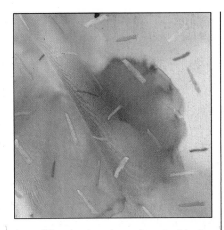

ABOVE: Silk paints have been allowed to bleed freely into the fine fabric and fabric crayons have then been used to apply a random pattern to the fabric which contrasts strongly to the gentle shapes created by the silk paints.

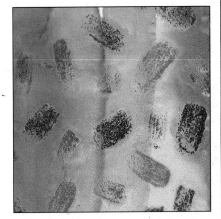

ABOVE: Silk paints have been sponged over silk, creating a rainbow effect. The fabric has then been left to dry and glitter paints have been dabbed onto its surface.

BEFORE YOU START

The advice given in this section is applicable to all types of painting, printing and dyeing and should always be carefully followed.

PREPARING YOUR WORK AREA

This will need some consideration and planning. A wide variety of techniques and approaches to design are set out in this book, and these should be thought about before you plan your work area. Less organization will be required by readers who have an area in the house which can be set aside for decorating fabrics. Those fortunate enough to be able to do this will be able to leave unfinished pieces of fabric in the work space without causing disruption to the rest of the household. Alternatively, a garage or workshed is ideal for fabric painting, as it will need less protection from stray splashes of paint which could be disastrous in a living room.

To allow the greatest freedom when executing a large piece of work, a garden or backyard is ideal, particularly if you are using a splash technique. Of course, this would be very much governed by the weather —working on a length of fabric outside with a rainstorm imminent could cause panic!

Many of us live in small flats or apartments where it is impossible to set aside a work area. Obviously, the task undertaken must then be appropriate to the space available. If necessary, small items such as napkins can be worked on one at a time. In order to attempt a larger piece of work, the necessary space must be organized. This might, for example, mean clearing a bedroom or living room of furniture so that the entire floor space can be used.

The importance of protecting the work area cannot be over-emphasized. Use old lengths of fabric or old sheets to cover all areas in the proximity of the work, rather as a painter or decorator would. If no fabric is available, newspapers, old wallpaper or lining paper can be used. It should not be necessary to spend any money on this, unless you are keen to set up a permanent textile work area. If this is the case, a length of medium to heavyweight cotton can be purchased. This can also serve as a backing cloth for fabric painting work, and can be washed and used over and over again.

If possible, it is useful to have a sink near the work space, as a constant supply of clean water will be needed If you are dyeing a fabric, it is best to avoid carrying dye baths long distances between the cooker and sink. The practical implications of the work you are considering must always be thought about carefully.

All necessary utensils and dyes must be kept near at hand. Protect the surface that they are standing on with lots of newspaper or a sheet of plastic. You will also need plenty of old rags, preferably cotton ones, to mop up spills and to wipe fingers and brushes.

PREPARING THE WORK TABLE

It is necessary to have a stable, flat table to work on. Its size will depend upon the size of fabric that you are going to print. Ideally, the table should have ample space for the fabric and the equipment to be used. If you do not have a large enough table, an old, flat door, placed on top of a smaller table or bench will make a fairly satisfactory work surface, but make sure that it is stable and will not topple over. When the door is not being used for fabric painting, it can be stored away, thereby saving space.

The working surface should be covered with an old blanket for padding, with a sheet laid over the top. It should be secured in position with tacks or tape, depending upon how permanent the work surface is to be. If the technique you are going to use does not require a padded surface, simply cover the table with old newspaper.

IDENTIFYING A FABRIC

When selecting a fabric for painting or dyeing, it is essential to establish whether it is constructed out of natural or man-made fibres. Although many fabric colours can be used on both types of material, certain dyes and paints are not compatible with both man-made and natural fibres. For instance, transfer crayons or paints produce the most vivid results when used on man-made, silky materials such as rayon, and fabric dyes will only give good results on 100% cotton.

Most good fabric shops will be able to give you the necessary information about the construction of a fabric. However, if you are planning to use a fabric you already have at home—for instance, if you wish to dye your bathroom towels—a simple test can be carried out by placing a thread from the material in contact with a naked flame. Natural fibres do not burn easily, and burning will stop as soon as the threads are removed from contact with the naked flame. It is important to realize that many woven fabrics are made from a mixture of fibres, and it may be necessary to test a number of warp and weft fibres. Obviously, this test should be carried out with great care and should not be attempted in a shop!

Having established the construction of the printing fabric, it is essential that you choose a dye or paint that is compatible with it. Using the wrong fabric paint will give disappointing results. All paints, pens, inks, dyes, etc., will clearly state which materials they are suitable for, and the importance of following the manufacturer's advice cannot be over-emphazised.

REMOVING THE MANUFACTURER'S FINISH

Most fabrics have been treated with special finishes to make them crisper, shinier, water resistant, etc. These finishes should be removed before printing or dyeing, as they will prevent the paint from being absorbed into the material, resulting in an uneven and unsatisfactory result. Most finishes can be removed by washing the fabric in ordinary soap powder. Cotton can be boiled for about thirty minutes in soapy powder and more delicate fabrics, such as wool and silk, should be left to soak in warm soap suds for about thirty minutes. The fabrics should then be thoroughly rinsed in cold water and dried away from direct heat or sunlight.

Alternatively, fabric can be bought which has been specially prepared for printing and dyeing. This fabric will not have been treated with any special finishes, and in some cases, it will have been bleached to improve the colour quality when dyed. Using fabric which has been specially prepared for printing and dyeing purposes will produce exceptionally lovely results.

If you are working on an old fabric, for instance bedlinen or a tablecloth, make sure that the fabric is perfectly clean before decorating it, because the paint will not take on dirty or greasy fabrics.

SELECTING A DYE/PAINT

Once you have selected and prepared the fabric that you are going to use, an appropriate fabric paint or dye must be chosen. There are more and more products available on the market, and it can be fun to experiment with different effects. Prepare samplers, using the fabric that you are going to work on to see how the paints, pens, crayons or dyes react to the material. This process is essential before you attempt the main project. However experienced you are with fabrics and dyes, you will find that unexpected results can occur. Certain fabrics may cause the colours to bleed more than you had expected, the colours may not dry to the shade that you had visualized, etc. It is, therefore, essential to produce samplers and miniatures of the main project, to avoid disappointment.

FIXING THE DYE

If the dye is not made permanent, the colour will run when the item is washed, and the colours will fade and become spoiled in sunlight, heat or by condensation. The majority of colours are fixed by applying heat to the fabric. The fabric paint manufacturer will give clear instructions for this process, and they should be carefully followed.

The most common way of fixing colour is to iron the printed or painted fabric on its reverse side for a few minutes. This is quick and simple when working on small to medium sized pieces of fabric. When you are using this process, the ironing board should be covered with a clean cloth to prevent any staining. A lightweight piece of cotton or a sheet of paper can be used for this purpose.

When working on larger lengths, it may be easier to apply the necessary heat by placing the fabric in a kitchen oven. The fabric should be folded neatly into a package. The package must fit into the oven without touching the top, bottom or sides. The folded fabric should be lightly wrapped in a piece of cotton or silver cooking foil, ensuring that all areas of the painted fabric are covered. The package should be left in the oven for about 7 minutes on 170°C (325°F).

Another alternative is to use a hairdryer to fix the paint. This method is suitable for items which cannot be ironed, such as lampshades. However, this can be a laborious process as the heat must be applied for many minutes, while taking great care not to scald the fabric with the hot air.

It is worthwhile preparing a number of small pieces of printed or painted fabric and experimenting with different fixing methods to establish which one is the most effective for the project you are undertaking. It is a great mistake to take short cuts with the fixing process. Loss of colour and detail will occur, and the design may be ruined when it is washed.

CLEANING THE FABRIC

If a design has been properly fixed, the colour will remain vivid when the item is washed. However, painted and dyed fabrics should be washed separately for the first couple of times to remove any loose particles of dye which will spoil the rest of the wash. Delicate fabrics, such as silk or wool, must always be gently hand-washed in warm water. If you do not feel confident that the colour will remain strong when the fabric is washed, it is advisable to have it dry-cleaned. However, if the colour is fixed properly in the first place, this expense should not be necessary.

It is a good idea for the novice to carefully wash all painted items by hand first, however securely the colour has been fixed. Once you are more experienced, you will know which paints and fabrics can be cleaned in a washing machine and which should be washed by hand or dry-cleaned.

Items such as lampshades, screens, very large wall hangings and blinds, which cannot be washed, can be kept clean by regular dusting or by vacuum cleaning. Items which have been varnished should be wiped clean with a damp cloth.

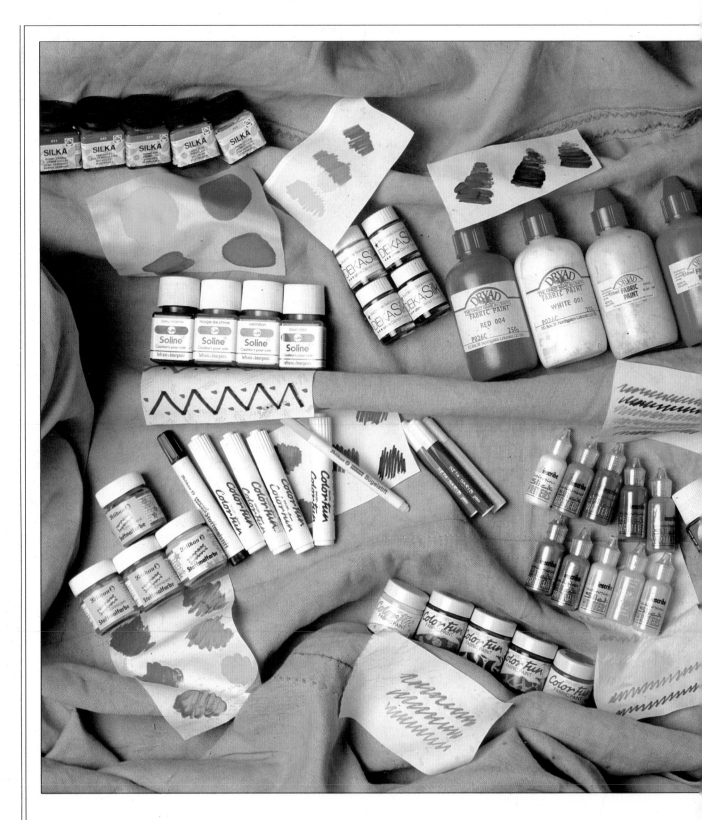

Fabric paints, pens and crayons are now available in an ever-increasing variety of guises. Illustrated in the picture are a selection of fabric paints, silk paints, glitter paints, fabric pens and heat-expanding paints.

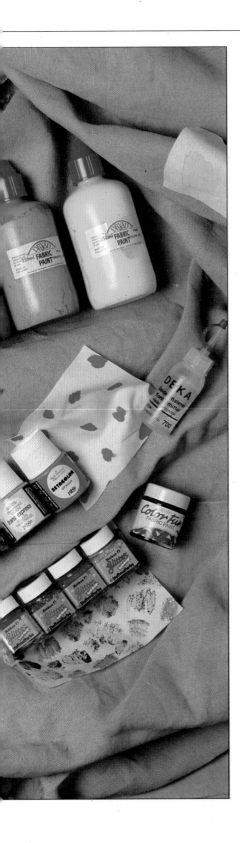

COLOUR MEDIUMS AND MATERIALS

The importance of using a fabric which is suitable for the project you are going to make cannot be over-emphasized. Its weight, texture, finish and compatibility to your design must all be taken into consideration. For instance, a large wall hanging must be executed on a heavy-weight material or it will not hang properly, and a flowery, delicate pattern for cushions will probably look most effective if it is executed on silk. Generally speaking, it is worthwhile buying good-quality fabrics for most items because the material will drape well and will have a longer life. However, cheaper man-made fabrics are suitable for transfer painting and can produce bright, fun results which can be used as pictures, wall pieces, window dressing or even cushions. Whatever material you decide to use, it is essential that the manufacturer's finish is removed before you paint.

Once you have decided upon your fabric, a paint medium must be selected which is suitable for the fabric and for the decorative method that you are planning to use. There are now many different ranges of pens and paints available, and this chapter will help you to understand how the basic types of fabric paints should be used and which materials they are compatible with. However, this section is only a guide to fabrics and paints. As your confidence grows, you will discover lots of exciting effects which can be achieved by combining a range of fabric paints within a design and by experimenting with different materials and techniques.

PAINTS

Today's modern paints and pens are all sold with clear manufacturer's instructions which should always be followed because the method of application and of making the paint permanent can vary enormously between different brands of paint.

Fabric pens and crayons are easy to use and are available in different thichnesses of nib. Heat-expanding paints and other textured paints are applied straight from the tube which requires some practice to obtain a controlled, even line of paint. Fabric paints and transfer paints are sold in bottles or jars and must be applied with a brush. For the beginner, an ordinary, cheap paint brush will be adequate for applying the paint, but a good quality sable brush will be easier to use and will give better results. You will probably want to build up a selection of different brush sizes. Fabric paints are water-soluble, so brushes should be rinsed thoroughly in clean water after use, and wiped dry with a clean cloth or tissue paper. Never leave a brush to stand in water—it will be ruined.

Fabric Dyes There are dyes available for both man-made and natural fabrics. It is essential that the correct type of dye is used for the material that you are going to dye, or pale, streaky results will occur. As a general rule, natural fabrics are well suited to dyeing, giving strong, clear colours, while man-made fabrics or mixes of say, polyester and cotton, will give paler results. There are two types of dye available; cold water dyes which are only suitable for natural fabrics such as cotton or linen, and hot water dyes, which can be used in the washing machine. However, certain washing machines are not suitable for this method as too much water passes through them, giving a pale end result.

The most satisfactory colours will be achieved when dyeing over a white or very pale fabric. If the material is dark, the resulting colour will be affected. It is not possible to dye a colour to a lighter shade, although fabrics can be bleached to remove their original colour and then over-dyed.

Fabric Crayons These crayons take on the same appearance when used on fabric as they do on paper, and are used in exactly the same way. Take great care not to smudge them as you are working. They are fixed in the same way as fabric paints, but do protect the iron with a clean cloth, as they can leave greasy marks. Fabric crayons can be used on any type of fabric and they can also be combined with other fabric paints for a more textural quality.

Fabric Paints These can be used on most fabrics. The available colour range is very large and compatible paints are intermixable to create an endless range of colours. All the paints can be diluted with water and are available in four finishes— pearlized, opaque, flourescent and transparent.

Different types of fabric paints react in different ways on material. For example, pearlized paints sit on the fabric and do not soak into it and for that reason, they can be used on darker backgrounds. White fabric paint can be mixed with opaque fabric paints to create pastel colours and will also remain on the surface of the cloth.

The amount of fabric paint necessary for a project will depend on the technique you are using and the amount of fabric to be painted. Techniques such as block-printing require very little paint and are therefore economical to produce. It is not necessary to buy every colour you want to use as colours can be mixed from a very limited range. Work this out before investing in any paints at all. Blend the colours in small pots or saucers, mixing minimal amounts to start with until you have produced the desired colour. When mixing a pastel shade, always add colour to white, not the other way around. Always mix enough paint to finish the job—any unused paint can always be stored for future use in an air-tight jar. Although fabric paint can be diluted, too much water will make the paint bleed into the fabric. This will not be appropriate if the desired effect is clean, straight lines. Therefore, the consistency of the paint must be suitable for the technique and for the material that it is being used on.

Fabric Pens These pens look and work like ordinary felt tip pens but are specially formulated to be used on fabric. They are available in two nib sizes—a fine tip and a wider tip. The pens can be used on most fabrics although the colour may bleed on a fine, smooth material. They are not suitable for use on fabrics with a dark background as the colour will not show up. When painted onto fabric, the pens give an effect which is rather like diluted fabric paint. They do have an advantage over fabric paints in that they are easier to control when painting fine lines and outlines. They are also ideal for painting in detailed stencils such as letters and numbers and can be used with any other type of fabric paint to highlight or outline areas. Fabric pens are not suitable for painting large flat areas, but are useful for scribbles, doodles and dots.

Glitter Paints Suitable for all surfaces, including paper, glitter paint is available in a wide range of colours and, as it remains on the surface of the fabric, can be used on darker backgrounds. It can be used to great effect with fabric paints.

Heat-Expanding Paints Bought in a tube, these opaque paints have a unique raised effect. These paints can be used on any type of fabric although fine fabrics are not suitable as the paint is too heavy. They are not recommended for use on fabrics that are washed frequently as the paint sits, slightly raised on the surface of the fabric. To apply the paint, gently press the nozzle of the tube onto the fabric. Apply more pressure if a thicker line is desired. For more solid areas a brush should be used. Leave the paint to dry, then turn the fabric over and iron the back for a few minutes with the iron set on a fairly hot temperature. The heat will expand the paint, making it raised and rubber-like in appearance. Wash the fabric carefully by hand.

Screen Printing Inks Most fabric paints can be used for screen printing, but it is more economical to use a thickening agent or a binder to spread the fabric paint so that it does not appear too thick on the fabric.

Industrial inks and paints are available in small quantities and will work out much cheaper if you are printing a large area of fabric. Screen printing inks are very concentrated and it is only necessary, therefore, to use a few drops to produce a strong colour. Always add the colour to a binder, as it is difficult to make the colour paler once it has been mixed. A white pigment will have to be added for a paler shade. All the printing inks are intermixable and water soluble, so the printing screen can be washed clean with water.

Silk Paints Especially made for painting onto silk, these paints are transparent and have a translucent quality. The colours may be thinned with water and can be mixed together to create other colours. Silk paints can often differ in the way that they are fixed — some are steam-fixed, others need ironing and some are immersed in a fixative solution. It is essential to read the manufacturer's instructions carefully when buying the paints and to buy the one that most suits you. Silk paints work well on wool as long as the wool is fine and smooth. Sometimes a diffusing agent is necessary to prevent the paint from drying too quickly and to stop any hard lines from appearing when covering large areas with a coat of paint. A diffusing agent can also be useful when merging colours into each other so that the paints gradually blend and do not have hard and definite edges where one colour stops and one starts.

Transfer Crayons These look like conventional crayons and are used in much the same way. However, like transfer paints, they are dull in appearance until they are transferred onto the fabric using an iron. Test each colour before starting to crayon your design. When ironing, cover the iron with paper or fabric so that the soft crayons do not mark the surface of the iron.

Transfer Paints These paints are only successful when used on man-made fabrics. When used on polyester cotton, the colours tend to be too pale, although this may be the desired effect. For vivid results use 100% polyester. The paints are available in individual pots or in sets. For the more ambitious, larger bottles are also available. All colours can be mixed together and diluted to form other tones and colours, but they are not compatible with other fabric paints. However, other fabric paints can be used in the same design. The colours of transfer paints can be misleading, as the paint in the bottle suggests dark dull tones. However when these paints are transferred onto fabric they take on quite a brilliant appearance. For this reason it is advisable to test each colour on a scrap of fabric before starting the finished design.

FABRICS

Most types of fabric, whether natural or synthetic, can be dyed, painted or printed. It is, however, important to check the manufacturer's instructions to ensure that the dye is suitable for the type of material you are planning to paint or print.

Natural fabrics accept most paints and dyes well and they are, of course, more luxurious to touch and to look at than synthetic materials. Man-made fabrics tend to imitate silks and cottons and are usually cheaper and easier to care for than natural fabrics, which crease more easily.

It is always a good idea to seek advice when buying a fabric in order to check whether it is made from 100% natural fibres like cotton or silk or from a fibre mix such as polyester/cotton. When buying synthetic materials, it is best to identify exactly what the fibres are, so that the appropriate dyes can be used. It is essential to read the instructions of any fabric printing colours, dyes or paints. By following these simple guidelines, the best results will be achieved. Using a printing colour which is incompatible with your fabric can result in real disappointment.

Whatever the material you select to work on, it is a good idea for the novice to practise on fabrics that are inexpensive, graduating to more luxurious ones when a few of the painting techniques have been mastered.

NATURAL FABRICS

COTTON
A wide variety of fabrics are made from cotton. Cotton fabrics offer an excellent media for painting. They absorb colour well in dyeing, and the range of different weights and weaves available gives a very wide selection of fabric surfaces and textures for printing and painting. It is a fairly inexpensive fabric.

Calico Also known as unbleached muslin, was first produced in India and is one of the world's oldest fabrics. It is a medium-weight fabric that often has a matt finish in its natural state. When untreated, its natural colour is creamy with brown flecks. Calico can be dyed easily, although the resulting colours are inclined to be rather dull. It is a firmly woven fabric, hard-wearing and cheap and is certainly recommended for the beginner for all types of fabric work. Calico can be purchased in a number of different weights, from lightweight and medium to quite heavyweight.

Cambric This material, sometimes known as 'chambray', is a fine, closely woven plain-weave fabric which sometimes has a slight shine to it. Once the shiny finish has been removed, the fabric takes dye well. However, uses in the home are limited as the fabric is very lightweight.

Canvas A heavy unbleached fabric, that is quite strong. It is often used by painters and is available in a variety of widths. A fairly inexpensive fabric but quite hard-wearing, it can successfully be used as a furnishing fabric for windows, as a throw-over on a sofa or for wall hangings. Being a firm, stable cloth, canvas is very good for hand-painting onto, but is unsuitable for dyeing.

Chintz This cotton fabric has a glossy finish and is usually known as 'glazed cotton'. It is often printed with birds or flowers and other traditional designs. When using chintz for printing or dyeing, you will need to remove the finish to give colour permanence, otherwise inconsistent results will occur. However, some fabric finishes will not wash out and it will retain a glazed appearance.

Damask This is an ancient type of fabric weave, first executed in silk from Damascus. It is now woven in cotton, linen and synthetics, and is available in many different weights. Its most common use is for table linen, and it can be printed on very successfully. It takes colour well and makes very elegant and hard-wearing tablecloths. Careful consideration ought to be given before using it for upholstery as damask creases easily.

Holland A plain-weave fabric usually made of cotton. When stiffened, this fabric is often used for making roller blinds and window shades. It takes fabric printing colour well. Firm and hard-wearing, rather like hessian or burlap, it is not very suitable for dyeing.

Lace This is an open-work fabric available in a variety of constructions.

Traditionally made from linen, it is now widely produced in cotton, polyester and nylon. The more decorative pieces of lace can look stunning at a window. Lace can be dyed if the fabric is 100% cotton. Printing and spraying onto cotton lace can be very effective. The different open constructions can also be sprayed through to give a delicate stencilled effect of lace on a plain cotton fabric.

Lawn This is a very fine, smooth fabric, which is sometimes known as 'calico'. It can be dyed and printed successfully, and is particularly attractive when used for making cushions or for general decoration in a bedroom.

Madras Cotton A soft cotton, also called madras muslin, this fabric is imported from the Far East. A fine and open-weave material which sometimes has other colours interwoven, it is an inexpensive fabric which is useful for practising and printing on. The additional colours can add surface interest when over-printing. It is not suitable for dyeing as the colours in the fabric are inclined to run.

Organdie This cotton fabric is quite crisp, almost transparent and very lightweight. It is ideal for use at windows, and takes dye well. It can be printed and hand-painted. The transparent quality of the fabric can be enhanced by using dyes without pigment. Fine spraying onto cotton organdie will produce lovely delicate effects for windows.

Percale This is a close-weave cotton, similar to poplin, that is usually used for continental quilt covers and other bedlinen. It is, therefore, available in a large variety of widths. It is suitable for printing, painting and dyeing.

Poplin A hard-wearing medium-weight fabric. It is traditionally made of cotton, although quite a lot is made with polyester and therefore creases less. It does have a slight sheen to it. A very durable and absorbent fabric, particularly suitable for printing and dyeing.

Sateen Cotton sateen has a sheen on the right side. It is a quite heavy fabric, often used for furniture and curtains. Its weight makes it unsuitable for dyeing but very good for printing and painting as the sateen finish creates a very luxurious effect.

Terry Towelling Towelling made of cotton can be painted on one or both sides, depending on the quality. It can be purchased in a variety of different colours as well as white. It can be dyed successfully, and printing, splashing and hand-painting can be used to decorate it.

Voile A soft, plain-weave fabric made in fine yarns, voile is very flimsy and semi-transparent. It can be used to great effect for draping at windows. Very suitable for dyeing, this lightweight cotton will produce excellent results. It can be used for all types of fabric printing and painting.

SILK
A natural fibre produced by silkworms, silk is used to make a great number of different types of fabrics. Most silks are extremely good for printing, painting and dyeing. Colour applied to silk is both rich and lustrous. Special dyes are available specifically for this fabric to retain its luxurious natural qualities. A slight bleed effect can occur with some silk, and it is always advisable to try out fabric colour on small samples to see how the dye bleeds on the fabric.

Chiffon A soft sheer fabric usually associated with evening dresses, chiffon can add a luxurious feel to a living area if used at a window. It does fray easily and can be difficult to sew. However, this silk fabric will take colour well in printing and painting.

Crepe de Chine A soft smooth silk that has a beautiful flowing quality and also has a slight sheen. It hangs beautifully, but is almost always used as a dress fabric. It is not particularly suited to dyeing, but will print well and can be purchased in an excellent range of colours.

Jap or Habutai A fine smooth silk which is usually used for linings. It is inexpensive and would be good for trying out silk paints. This fabric can be bought in a variety of different weights from light and medium to heavy. An excellent fabric for painting and printing, it will also dye beautifully. It takes colour well and the lustre of the fabric enhances the richness of dye colours.

Shantung This slubbed silk has a slightly textured appearance, with a delicate sheen and a luxurious feel to it. The slub effect in the material adds surface interest. It takes colour well and can be used for printing and painting.

Taffeta A stiff silk that rustles when moved. The most expensive type is one that is made from two colours and seems to change colour in the light. Taffeta is usually associated with dress fabric, but is beautiful when used as a furnishing fabric, although it is very expensive. Some bleeding effects can occur on this silk when painted or printed.

Tulle A fine silk net, tulle looks beautiful when bunched together. A much more common version is made of polyester, although it does not have such a fairy-tale quality. Interesting effects can be achieved by printing over a double layer of fabric. Silk fabric with a silk tulle overlay that is printed or painted will give a marvellous shimmering effect when hung together. Because of the open net effect, designs should be simple. Spraying can produce beautiful light, delicate results.

Tussah This material is commonly known as 'wild silk'. This is a thick textured fabric, not unlike hessian (burlap) with an uneven slub. An interesting and less lustrous material than most silks, it is a good fabric for printing on.

Twill A weave with a diagonal stripe, twill is usually woven in silk but can be woven in any fabric including cotton. Again, this silk will take colour well in printing and painting, but might be inclined to bleed because of its woven structure.

Voile When made of silk, this fabric has a rough texture and is usually available in cream with flecks of brown. Its texture gives a pleasing surface effect when printed. The cream background colour has little effect on the printing colour.

LEATHER
This is an animal hide or skin, and can be decorated with coloured leather shoe dyes for interesting effects.

LINEN
Linen is a natural fibre made from flax. A woven fabric, it is available in a wide variety of weights. It is suitable for both dress and furnishing fabrics. It is expensive and creases badly, but this is all part of its charm. Linen takes dye and fabric paint very well.

VELVET
A pile cloth made of silk, cotton or polyester. It takes both dye and fabric paint very well. Always use silk paints on silk velvet.

WOOL
This fabric is warm, luxurious and comes in many guises, but is not usually associated with fabric painting, although wool challis is an ideal surface for fabric paint, as it is fine and smooth. Thicker wools are suitable for dyeing, but are too textured for painting or printing, although knitting yarn takes dye very well.

MAN-MADE FABRICS

ACETATE
This man-made fibre can be mixed with a variety of other fibres including cotton viscose and nylon. It has good draping qualities for furnishing and can be printed or coloured with transfer inks.

INTERFACING
This is usually used in dressmaking to reinforce fabrics. It is an inexpensive fabric which can be bought on the roll and is either a woven or non-woven fabric. A variety of fabric colours, including silk paints and dyes can be applied to the fabric for very exciting results. However, this fabric is really only suitable for wall hangings or as pictures, once it has been decorated.

NYLON
A sheer fabric usually used as net curtains. It is cheap and hard-wearing, but is not a particularly stylish fabric. It is often resistant to chemicals. Although some dyes are specifically prepared for nylon, only light to medium colours can be achieved. Car spray paints can be used successfully on nylon fabric.

POLYESTER
The most common of man-made fabrics this fabric is also known as 'rayon'. It is able to imitate many natural fabrics very well and has the added advantage of being much cheaper. It washes well and is often mixed with natural fibres. It is most suitable for transfer paints and crayons, giving lovely, vivid effects.

Polyester (Rayon) Cotton This fabric is made from a blend of natural cotton fibres and polyester. This makes the fabric more hard-wearing and it is commonly used. It is most suitable for all fabric printing and dyeing although, as always, the correct type of dye or paints must be used. The percentage of polyester can vary greatly as the fabric is made in a good range of different weights.

Polyester (Rayon) Crepe A soft fabric, which is very hard-wearing. This fabric can be used for printing, but is best used for transfer printing colours. The intense colour of transfer inks work best on 100% polyesters of all types.

Polyester (Rayon) Satin This fabric has a satin sheen and works well with transfer inks. The sheen will give the painted fabric an interesting, luminous quality.

Polyester Sheer This firm net fabric has a hard quality. It can be coloured with transfer inks. Used with imagination, it can make an interesting effect at a window, particularly when the light shines through the fabric.

PVC
This is a chemically-made material which is known as 'vinyl' in North America. Its full name is polyvinyl chloride. Most fabrics called 'PVC' have a fabric base which has been coated. There are a variety of uses for this fabric, in and out of doors. Special fabric colours can be applied from puff pens, which will dry and stick to the PVC.

ULTRASUEDE
An imitation suede which is hard to distinguish from the real thing. Particularly exciting results can be achieved when it is decorated with transfer paints.

RIGHT: This fine art hanging by Jacqueline Guille has been executed on a fine silk fabric using silk paints.

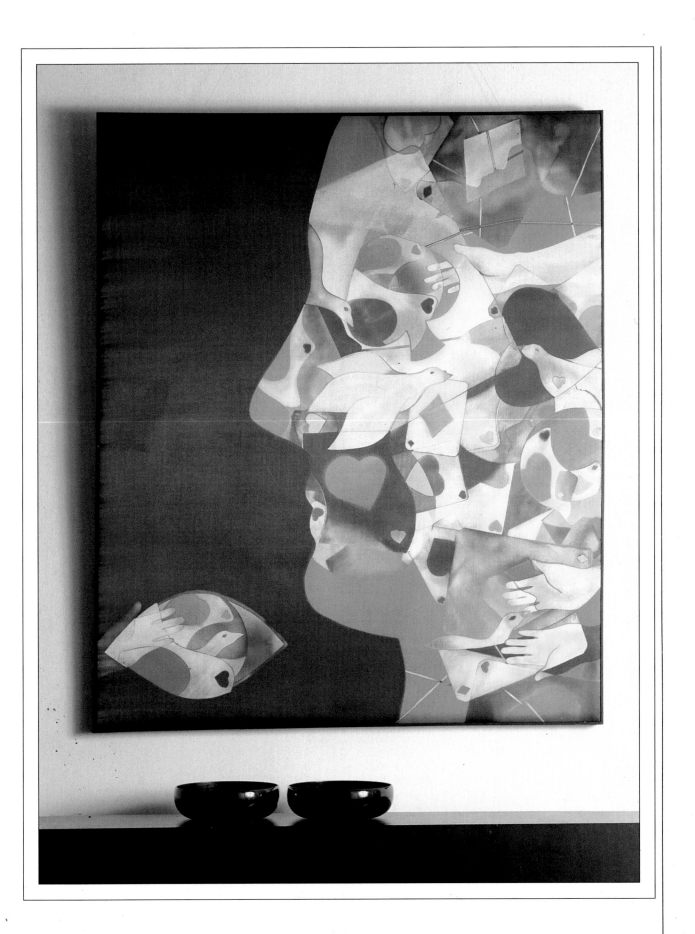

These stylish throw-overs have been decorated using very basic printing techniques.
Ideal for the beginner to tackle, printing these drapes will teach the novice
a great deal about fabric and how to paint it.

LIVING

The living area provides endless opportunities for fabric painting designs and experiments, from the subtle to the outrageous. A bland, uninteresting decor can be transformed by introducing imaginative soft furnishings—an African-style wall hanging painted in rich browns and ochre will exude an exotic warmth into your home. Stencilled, sponged or spattered drapes flung over existing furniture will restore life to even the most tired sofa, and hand-painted scatter cushions will add a focal point to dreary decor.

A great deal of time is spent in the living room and its functions are usually diverse—a study, a reading room, a television room, an entertainment area. It is therefore important to consider the atmosphere you wish to create before embarking upon costly, time-consuming projects. Do you want the area to be cool and neutral or do you want to introduce strong, individual themes? Available light and space must also be taken into account to maintain the overall balance of the room.

When considering your textile design, you may wish to exploit the existing decor in the room. For example, a motif in the carpet or curtains could be simplified and translated onto the cushion covers. Alternatively, the colours in a striking painting or poster could be transferred onto a hand-painted item to introduce continuity to the room's decor.

Inspiration for fabric design can be taken from any source and is limited only by your own imagination. Artistic ability should not be an inhibiting factor — so many interesting patterns can be created at random and faithful reproduction of an existing print or picture should not be attempted by the amateur artist as it is never wholly successful.

Scatter cushions are relatively quick and inexpensive items to produce for the living room and are therefore ideal for beginners. Once you are a little more experienced, larger projects such as curtains and furnishing drapes can be tackled. Remember that an aborted project can often be transformed into a picture or small wall hanging!

More ambitious items such as screens and large wall hangings can be demanding and the materials costly. They require time and, depending upon the technique chosen, experience. However, the effort is usually worthwhile. The end result will be completely different to anything that could be purchased in a shop and it will be a satisfying tribute to your skill, imagination and artistry.

BLACK AND WHITE THROW-OVERS

Texture is the key to block printing and the combination of black and white fabrics and paints dramatically demonstrate this. Complementary colours, for instance ochre and brown, are also very effective.

For these throw-overs, two types of block printing were used—rope and potato.

EQUIPMENT FOR POTATO PRINTS

lengths of cotton or cotton jersey
potato
fabric paints
masking tape
tailor's chalk
clean saucers
household paint brush
fabric paints
clean cloth for ironing
iron to fix the paint

BELOW: Many varied and interesting effects can be achieved by printing onto fabric with cut potato shapes.

METHOD USING POTATO PRINTS

1 Experiment with the cut potato trying out various shapes until you find a motif that is pleasing.

2 Cover the flat side of the potato with a thin film of paint. Do not use too much paint or you will create thick, uneven borders of paint around the print.

3 Press the potato firmly onto the fabric. Repeat the prints over the fabric, reapplying paint on alternate prints. Leave the fabric to dry.

4 Fix the dye in place by ironing the painted side of the fabric with a hot iron, placing a cloth between the fabric and the iron.

TIPS

o *Leave the cut potato to dry for half an hour before printing. This will get rid of any excess moisture in the potato which would make the print too watery.*

EQUIPMENT FOR ROPE BLOCKS

lengths of cotton or cotton jersey
rope
wooden blocks
strong glue
masking tape
tailor's chalk
clean saucers
fabric paints
selection of paint brushes
clean cloth for ironing
iron to fix the paint

METHOD USING ROPE BLOCKS

1 Experiment with different types of rope—a skipping rope is ideal—until you find a suitable texture. Making rough sketches of coil shapes and wiggles will help you to create the motif you want.

2 Cover the surface of the wooden block with glue and stick the rope down onto it in the shape of the motif. Make sure that it is firmly stuck down. Leave to dry.

3 Stretch the fabric out onto your working surface and secure it down firmly with masking tape.

4 If the motifs are to be repeated over the fabric in a random pattern, precise planning of where they will fall is not necessary. If the motifs are to be repeated in a set pattern, work out where each motif should be printed and mark the place on the fabric with tailor's chalk.

5 Pour the paints into the saucers to avoid overloading the brush.

6 Paint the surface of the rope using a brush which is just wide enough to cover the rope. Do not use too much paint or the textures of the rope will disappear when the motif is printed.

7 Repeat the prints over the fabric. Print alternate motifs to minimize the possibility of the paint smudging. Reapply the fabric paint for every other printing so that the rope block does not get overloaded. Leave the fabric to dry.

8 Fix the dye in place by ironing the painted side of the fabric with a medium hot iron, placing a cloth between the fabric and the iron.

TIPS

o *Use undiluted fabric paint for block printing. If the paint is watered down it will bleed into the material.*

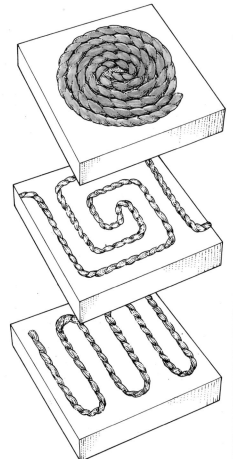

ABOVE: These blocks with coiled rope glued to each printing surface, are used for rope block printing. The blocks can be used again and again, experimenting with different colourways on fabrics. There is no need to work only with black and white (left)—complementary colours, such as the examples of black, brown and red on mustard can also be very effective (right).

37

ORIENTAL SILK DRAPES

The rich lustre and texture of real silk cannot be equalled. It is a particularly satisfying fabric to work on because it has a delicate, translucent quality not found in other materials. Cushions, drapes, wall hangings and pictures are all ideal mediums for displaying hand-painted silk and they will add an air of opulence to your decor.

Fabric paints specially manufactured for painting on silk must always be used. Because they soak into the fabric, they will retain the translucent quality of the material, whereas other fabric dyes will give the cloth a dull, opaque finish which is not satisfactory.

Silks are available in a variety of weights and weaves, but it is advisable to select a fairly fine weave without any slubs. This will enable you to create an even texture of paint over the material without any ugly areas of heavily concentrated colour.

Natural silk (cream) or bleached silk (white) should be chosen. Because silk paints soak into the fabric, they will be lost on a dark colour. Pastel shades and pale grey can be used, but the colour of the fabric will affect the tone of the paints.

Before you start on your main project, experiment on small sample pieces of the type of silk you are going to use to see precisely how the paint bleeds into the fabric.

For this fabric, flower forms were freely interpreted, using a full range of clear, bright colours. The paints were allowed to blend freely into each other within the gutta outlines.

RIGHT: These drapes have a richness of colour which is unique to silk painting. The bright, exotic shapes and colours combine to create a bold, dramatic effect.

TIPS

o *When painting silk, the paints will blend more freely if the fabric is elevated from the work surface. This will stop the paint from soaking through the material and into the protective sheet or paper beneath it. The intensity of the colour will be stronger too. The best way of doing this is by stretching the material over a wooden frame, making sure that the edges of the frame are perfectly smooth and will not snag the material.*

EQUIPMENT

fine silk
soft pencil
wooden frame to work on (optional)
masking tape
silk paints
clean saucers
gutta
selection of artist's brushes
clean cloth for ironing
iron for fixing the paint

METHOD

1 Select the colours you are going to use by preparing preliminary fabric samplers to see how they blend into each other and the material.

2 Mark your design on the fabric using a soft pencil.

3 Prepare your work surface, securing the fabric firmly down on it with masking tape. Make sure that the fabric is taut and will not slip.

4 Prepare the paints. If you want to blend colours or water them down, this should be done in clean saucers. Remember that the paints will bleed much more freely into the fabric if they are watered down.

5 Apply the gutta along the areas of fabric where you want to create a border of undyed silk between the colours. Allow the gutta to dry thoroughly before applying any paint.

6 Apply the paints one at a time, starting with the palest colour. Wash and dry your brush thoroughly between each application. If you want to minimize the bleed effects, leave each colour to dry before applying the next.

7 To create a colour mix over the paints you have already applied, fresh coats of colour can be painted over the fabric, once it has dried.

8 When completely dry, remove the fabric from the work surface and fix the paints by slowly ironing the whole surface of the silk with a medium hot iron. Cover the ironing board and the silk with thin paper or fabric prior to ironing.

9 Wash the silk gently in luke-warm soap suds to remove the gutta, allowing it to soak briefly first.

10 Dry the silk and iron with a warm iron to remove any creases.

stencilling

WHITE ON WHITE SILK CURTAIN

Curtains and blinds are an ideal medium for displaying your hand-executed fabric designs to their full advantage. Not only is the fabric seen over a large area, but our eyes are naturally drawn towards the light of a window.

White silk paint used on white semi-transparent fabric produces a subtle but sophisticated effect which is enhanced when light filters through the fabric. This technique is particularly successful when used within a colourful decor.

RIGHT: Opaque white fabric paint is used to stencil a simple repeating shape onto semi-transparent silk. Although the fabric is the same colour as the paint, the pattern will still be prominent on the silk, particularly when the sun shines through the window. Alternatively, a contrasting colour can be used on white (see below) for a stronger impact.

EQUIPMENT

jap silk or cotton voile
masking tape
white multi-purpose fabric paint
clean saucers
stencil card or acetate
scalpel or craft knife
artist's brush
clean cloth for ironing
iron for fixing the paint

METHOD

1 Stretch out as much of the fabric as possible onto your working surface using masking tape to secure it down. Fine fabrics do tend to slip more easily, so ensure that it is firmly and tautly held in place.

2 Use the fabric paint undiluted. Pour it onto a plate or saucer. This will prevent the brush from becoming overloaded with paint.

3 Draw a simple zig-zag shape onto the centre of a sheet of stencil card or acetate. Cut out the shape using a craft knife.

4 Place the card on the fabric. Using one hand to keep the stencil firmly in position, paint in the stencil using a dabbing action.

5 Leave the stencil in place for a few seconds until the paint is almost dry, then remove it. Ideally you should wait until each motif is absolutely dry before removing the stencil, but when painting the same motif many times it is not practical to allow each one to dry.

6 Reposition the stencil onto another part of the fabric. Not many of us have enough space to stretch out long lengths of fabric, so paint the cloth in sections, waiting for each section to dry before working on the next one. Try to arrange the motifs so that, although they are randomly stencilled on the fabric, the spacing is fairly even.

7 Repeat the above process until all of the fabric has been painted. Leave the fabric to dry thoroughly on a flat surface.

8 Fix by ironing onto the painted side of the fabric with a hot iron.

TIPS

o *The paint will seep through the fabric onto your working surface. Cover the table with old sheets or a blanket before securing the fabric down for painting. Do not use newspaper as this will leave dirty smudges on the fabric.*

paints, pens and crayons

COMPLEMENTARY PICTURE AND CUSHION

The silk cushion and picture are not identical, but their fine lines and delicate tones relate strongly to each other. It is important to experiment with the colours you are going to use so that the pieces complement each other and their setting.

Although silk paints should normally be used on silk, ordinary multi-purpose fabric paints have been used for the cushion and picture because a dull finish without any bleed into the fabric was desired for this design.

EQUIPMENT FOR PICTURE

fine silk
masking tape
fabric paints
clean saucers
household paintbrush
fabric felt tip pens
clean cloth for ironing
iron to fix the paints

THE PICTURE

1 Any fabric can be used for this picture but heavier materials may not fit easily behind the frame. Stretch the fabric out over your working surface, fixing it down firmly at the edges with masking tape. If you want to create a crumpled effect, use a piece of fabric which is about twice the size of your frame.

2 Mix the colour you want to use, beginning with white and gradually adding to it until you achieve the strength of colour that you require. Using a household paintbrush, dip it lightly into the paint so that the brushstrokes are dry and the texture of the strokes are clearly shown.

3 Paint the more definite shapes using darker colours. Keep all the fabric paints quite separate, washing and drying the brush before using another colour. Fabric paint that is too wet or applied with a dirty brush will spoil the design as the colours will be murky.

4 When the paints have dried, apply the felt tip pens. The pens will add a linear quality to the design with squiggles, dots and dashes. They work just as well over fabric paint as they do on unpainted fabric. They are also easy to control when drawing lines and outlining.

5 When the design is perfectly dry, place a cloth over the picture and fix the paints by ironing with a hot iron for a few minutes.

TIPS

o *When using fabric crayons, keep the fabric taut so that they are easier to apply. Be careful not to smudge the crayons or press too hard as they can easily break up and spoil the fabric.*

o *Always place paper between the crayonned fabric and the iron when fixing the design, as the wax could easily mark your iron. Once fixed, the crayons will not smudge.*

EQUIPMENT FOR CUSHION

silk cushion cover
masking tape
fabric paints
clean saucers
household paintbrush
fabric crayons
lighter fluid
clean cloth for ironing
iron to fix the paints

THE CUSHION

1 Place a protective sheet of paper between the front and the back of the cushion cover to prevent paint from seeping through and spoiling the back of the cushion.

2 The cushion is painted in the same way as the wall hanging, using a shade of brown which is complementary to the violet in the picture. Fabric crayons have been used to highlight areas of the design. The edges of the crayon have been softened by applying a small amount of lighter fluid. This breaks down the waxy surface, causing the colour to bleed into the fabric, creating a shaded area.

3 Fix the design in the same way as for the picture.

LEFT: An abstract design combining paints and crayons is used on both the cushion and the silk picture to create a soft, harmonious mood.

ABSTRACT SCREEN

This design has been painted onto a ready-made screen, the stretched canvas being an ideal surface to work on. The heavy frame lends itself to a strong, geometric design. A work on this large a scale as needs careful forward planning as any mistakes will result in having to remove the canvas and replace it with a new piece. Before you start, make lots of rough sketches, trying out different colour combinations and cutting out the design shapes to scale. Play around with the shapes, moving them into different positions until a satisfactory arrangement is found.

EQUIPMENT

screen
paper
soft pencil
selection of brushes
gesso
fine sandpaper (optional)
acrylic paints
clean saucers
clean rags and paper

TIPS

o *If the paint looks patchy, leave it to dry and then paint another coat over it.*

o *Make sure that the design is centralized on each piece of canvas, so that the panels co-ordinate with each other.*

o *If you are not happy with a colour tone or area of design, simply leave it to dry, then paint over it. The original colour will not affect the new shade.*

METHOD

1 Prime the canvas with gesso. Gesso has been used for centuries for this purpose as it provides a perfect surface for paints. Apply the gesso with a wide brush. About four coats will be necessary.

2 If a smooth finish is required, the gesso should be gently sanded down. However, for this screen, the gesso has been incorporated into the design and left with a slight texture.

3 Acrylic paints are intermixable and water soluble. Blend all the colours beforehand, making sure that you have mixed enough paint to finish the screen, as colour matching may be difficult and time-consuming.

4 Draw the design over the top of the gesso, using a pencil, then fill in the shapes using the acrylic paints and an appropriately sized brush. Complete each panel before starting on the next one.

5 Leave the canvas to dry. These paints do not need fixing.

RIGHT: *Inspired by the spontaneous patterning of ink blobs of colour, the shapes have been enlarged and transferred onto canvas using strong, complementary colours.*

ABORIGINAL SCREEN

Screens today do not usually have a solely practical function—they are often purely decorative, having the same role to play in a room as a print or a painting. Neither do they have to be decorated with the floral patterns of the past—abstract and geometric designs are just as acceptable in complementary surroundings.

This screen was inspired by the elemental painting of Australian Aboriginal art and mixed with motifs from the world of graphics to produce a work that is a cross-fertilization of techniques and inspirations.

EQUIPMENT

screen
gesso
wide household brush
fine sandpaper (optional)
rope
acrylic spray paint
images for collage
acrylic gel medium

METHOD

1 Prime the canvas panels with gesso using a wide household brush. This will prevent paint from seeping through to the other side of the canvas. It will also provide a harder, less absorbent surface to work on.

2 If a smooth finish is required, rub the gesso down with fine sandpaper once it has dried. For this screen, the gesso has been incorporated into the design and left with a slight texture.

3 To achieve the background pattern, lay pieces of loosely coiled rope over the canvas. Spray over the canvas with an acrylic spray paint, so that when the rope is removed, its patterns will be left on the canvas.

4 The images on the screen are, of course, a matter of personal preference. Photographs, pictures from magazines and postcards can all be used to form your own unique design. In this case, all the images, except for the postcard, were photocopied onto a fine paper using a colour copier. Alternatively, black and white film stills or cuttings from newspapers can be used to give an interesting result. The possibilities are endless.

5 Apply the images to the canvas by soaking them in a watered-down acrylic gel medium. Gesso cannot be used as it will leave an opaque finish over the pictures. Stick the pictures to the canvas, then build up further coats of gel to the whole area of canvas. This will provide a protective cover as well as producing a seamless interface between the canvas and the images.

RIGHT: A combination of primitive motifs and contemporary collage imagery is used on this screen. Dusty, soft colours with a hint of brights, are painted onto the canvas, giving a highly original flavour to a very traditional piece of furniture.

DECORATIVE ROSES

The same motif can be used on several items in a room to great effect. It will unify the decor as well as introducing an attractive design feature.

In this case, the rose motif was used on a floor rug, cushion, chair and drape. The same motif has been used throughout, but with simple variations in both design and colour so that it does not become tedious to the eye. Adjusting the size of the pattern according to what you are going to paint it onto, can also be successfully used.

The colours for this design have been carefully selected to look fresh and bright, without being gaudy. The paints have therefore been toned down with white, giving them a subtle, slightly chalky appearance, more appropriate to this design than harsher tones. The simplest motifs can look stunning when painted in carefully thought out colours.

It is always worthwhile spending time mixing and experimenting with paints on the fabric you are actually going to use before embarking upon the main project. Try out lots of different colour combinations — sometimes the most unlikely shades can look stunning together when used in an appropriate design. Remember that fabric paint takes on a less intense colour once it has thoroughly dried, so let the test strips of fabric dry before deciding upon your final design.

For this project, where the different fabrics vary in thickness, texture and shade, it is particularly important to colour-test each surface, because the paints will alter according to the fabric. For instance, the pink of the rug will be more intense than that painted on the chair, simply because the fabric on the chair is darker than that on the rug.

When experimenting with colour, it is essential to keep notes of how each colour was mixed, as it may be difficult to find the right combination again. It is also important to mix plenty of paint for the actual project, as mixing an identical colour is almost impossible, even when careful notes are followed.

Remember to use paints which are appropriate to the fabric you are decorating. If you are working on silk, for instance a silk cushion cover or silk drape, silk paints must be used. Ordinary fabric paints will give the fabric a dull quality. Again, lots of experiments are essential, to ensure that the colour tones of each design complement each other.

The colours used for this particular interior are quite cool and brittle, all with a very subtle hint of blue in them. This type of colour palette gives an immediate impression of formal sophistication to the decor, combined with a light, fresh Mediterranean feeling. The combination of colours — citrus yellow, ice blue, emerald green and fuschia blend beautifully together to create an elegant refined mood. They also give an impression of air and space, ensuring that furnishings do not become too oppressive or dominant within a room setting. However, many people find these types of cooler colours disturbing to live with, preferring earthy, natural shades which can certainly be more soothing and relaxing in the home. These types of colours include shades of brown, deep reds, oranges, cream and certain yellows. Earthier colours can make a room appear to be smaller, whilst giving an impression of comforting warmth. The type of colour palette you decide to use is, of course, a matter of personal choice.

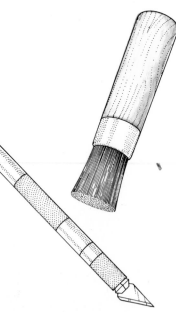

ABOVE: It is worthwhile investing in a good quality craft knife and stencil brush. As well as being easy to handle, using the correct equipment will ensure a clean edge to the motifs and an even coverage of paint.

EQUIPMENT

canvas for rug
cotton cushion cover
canvas chair
length of cotton fabric
paper and pencil
acetate
glass surface for cutting
craft knife or scalpel
masking tape
fabric paints
clean saucers
stencil brush
tailor's chalk
clean cloth for ironing
iron for fixing the paint

GENERAL METHOD

1 Work out your design, preparing drawings to scale to ensure that the designs work together as a group, as well as individually.

2 Each motif must be prepared as a separate stencil. The triangles are the same size on each piece of fabric, so the same stencil can be used for all surfaces. Two sizes of leaf and two sizes of flower have been used. These motifs can be enlarged or reduced by using a grid.

3 The stencils should be cut out of acetate rather than stencil card

because it is transparent. Place the acetate over your finalized drawing and fix it down firmly onto a cutting surface using masking tape. A glass cutting surface is smoother than wood and will ensure that the stencil has clean edges.

4 Cut the pattern out of the acetate using a craft knife. When cutting the rose stencils make sure that the 'bridges' are not too fine or they will break when they become wet.

5 Mix all the colours in clean saucers, making sure that you have enough to complete each project. To achieve the colours used in this design, white was used to tone down the paints and give a slightly chalky appearance. By using white as a base colour, all the colours will appear to be the same, even when the background fabric is slightly darker. Add colour to the white paint until the correct tone for the fabric is achieved.

6 Once each project has been completed, allow the paints to dry. Fix the paints onto the fabric by ironing on the painted side of the fabric with a medium hot iron, placing a cloth between the fabric and the iron.

TIPS

o *The motifs will be more effective if they have a grainy quality and are not simply solid shapes. To achieve this effect, use a perfectly dry stencil brush with a small amount of undiluted fabric paint on its tip.*

o *When painting the straight lines using masking tape, don't be tempted to remove the masking tape before the paint is dry. The paint could easily smudge or bleed as it is removed, causing the edge to be uneven.*

o *Cut the stencils out of fairly large pieces of acetate, leaving plenty of acetate around the pattern in order to easily manoeuvre the stencil on the fabric. This will also minimize the risk of the stencil tearing.*

o *If you are cutting the stencil on a glass surface, cover the edges of the glass with several layers of masking tape.*

BELOW: The same stencil can be used for different colours to create a variety of effects. Remember to wash it thoroughly before changing the paint.

THE CUSHION

1 Place a protective cloth inside the cushion cover to prevent paint from seeping through onto the back of the cushion.

2 Using tailor's chalk, mark where the motifs should be placed.

3 Stencil the small leaf and a flower. Although this is on a much smaller scale, repeat the same process as on the rug for the lines and the triangles.

THE CANVAS CHAIR

1 Remove the chair's canvas back and seat before stencilling.

2 Use the edges of the back and the seat as guidelines to ensure that the stencils are positioned centrally. You may want to cut a new stencil for the complete row of roses. Although this will take longer, it will ensure that they are stencilled in exactly the right position, which is vital on this relatively small piece of fabric.

THE CURTAIN

1 As this is a very strong design, it is not necessary to cover the whole curtain with motifs. A border is all that is necessary to co-ordinate it with the rest of the fabrics.

2 Again, make sure that all the guidelines are present, using either tailor's chalk or a very light pencil mark.

3 Stencil the rows of triangles first, then the flowers, followed by the leaves.

THE CANVAS RUG

1 Mark where each motif should be on the fabric by measuring in from each edge, allowing enough fabric to be turned under.

2 Place the large floral stencil in one corner. Dip the brush into the paint very lightly, so that it is almost dry. With a dabbing action known as 'pouncing', paint in the stencil. Leave to dry, then remove the stencil and wipe it clean.

3 Repeat in all four corners. Wash the brush and leave it to dry.

4 Position the leaf stencil at the side of one of the flower motifs. Stencil in the leaf, using the same method as for the rose.

5 Link the motifs with a straight border, using tailor's chalk as a guideline. Use two strips of masking tape and paint between them. When the paint is completely dry, remove the masking tape.

6 Place the triangle stencil inside the straight line and stencil all the way around the edge of the rug.

7 To complete the design, cut one triangle motif out of acetate and stencil a few triangles randomly around the rug. Do not use too many, or you will spoil the 'fresh' look of the rug.

RIGHT: Flowers have always been widely used in fabric design, whether for clothes or for interiors. Appealing to our basic love of the countryside, they introduce a fresh, timeless quality to decoration. Here, the stencilled roses provide an interesting contrast to the strong, geometric shapes used in the design.

freestyle painting

AFRICAN WALL HANGING

For a hanging as large as this one, a heavyweight canvas should be used. The woven structure of the cloth becomes an important textural element in the pattern, adding to its ethnic quality.

The designs for this hanging were based on African geometric textile designs from tribal garments and masks. The overall effect has been achieved by building up panels and sections using simple shapes such as squares, oblongs and triangles. The design has been encased in a strong black border to link all the elements together.

To achieve an earthy colour tone, the use of dyes has been strictly limited to three colours—yellow, black and red. The variations to these basic colours have been achieved by blending them or by using white to lighten and black to darken the shades.

All colours should be mixed in advance following trials and experiments on paper. Work on a strip of canvas for an accurate indication of how the colours will work. Mix the lightest colours first, i.e. the yellow, orange and mustard tones in clean saucers. Gradually add darker colours by blending combinations of the three main colours—yellow, red and black. Keep water and clean rags near at hand to clean the brushes. Place a small blob of colour down on the test strip and methodically lay each colour down until you have mixed the full range of colours. By placing the colours next to each other the contrasts and effects can be clearly seen and considered before embarking upon the actual hanging.

EQUIPMENT

heavyweight canvas
fabric paints
clean containers for mixing the paints
clean rags
soft pencil
selection of brushes
tin foil
clean jar of water

METHOD

1 Prepare your working area, making sure that you have plenty of room to work around the hanging. It is not necessary to secure a large, heavy canvas like this onto a work surface as it will not move around.

2 Mix your colours in clean saucers, making sure that you have enough paint to complete each area.

3 Draw the design lightly onto your fabric using a pencil.

4 To prevent smudging, start painting at the top of the fabric, working downwards. The lightest colours—yellows and oranges—should be used first. Step back from the fabric after completing each section to ensure that you are achieving the right effect.

5 The textured effect in the central area of the hanging is achieved by making spots and circles over the fabric and simply dragging a dry brush over the area.

6 Once you have reached the bottom edge of the fabric, step back to view the overall effect. You may want to emphasize certain areas in black or create stippled effects with paint over certain colour blocks.

7 Once you are completely satisfied, allow the fabric to dry overnight.

8 Fold the fabric neatly, turning it in on itself so that no painted areas are exposed. Wrap it up in tin foil then place it in a preheated oven set on 180°C (350°F) for seven minutes. Allow it to cool before unwrapping it. This will have fixed the paint.

9 The fabric is now ready for hanging. Any creases will drop out once the fabric is in position.

TIPS

o If you make a mistake while laying the colours, a light shade can be painted over. If you want to correct a dark shade, leave it to dry, then cover it with white paint. The new colour can be placed over the white base. It is not advisable to follow this procedure unless it is really necessary as the surface of the fabric becomes clogged with layers of paint and its texture is lost.

o Probably the best method of hanging a piece of fabric of this size and weight is to secure it to wooden poles top and bottom.

o It is advisable to cover work surfaces with lining paper, newspaper or inexpensive fabric. If you decide to work on the floor, allowance must be made for access around your fabric, should retouching or reworking areas be necessary. Fabric colour needs time to dry and should really be left overnight, so bear this in mind when selecting your working space. If the weather is warm and guaranteed not to rain, a garden or backyard is an ideal place to paint the wall hanging, as the sun will speed up the drying process.

The powerful images of African tribal art and decoration have been used for inspiration when designing this hanging. A series of sketches, experimenting with colours and shapes, were drawn using wax crayons before deciding upon the finished design.

silk paints

CUSHION COVERS

Piles of beautiful, hand-painted cushions always create a impression of luxury, especially when the cushion covers have been fashioned out of a good quality silk, as these ones have been. It is not advisable to use very fine silk or one which will crease easily, as the cushion covers will probably have to stand up to quite a lot of wear and tear in the living room.

The ornate, rather formal motifs on this series of silk cushion covers was carefully thought out to enhance the room's restful but traditional decor. Although each cushion cover has a separate design, they complement each other as a group, creating a feeling of both movement and continuity.

A soft, powder blue was selected to enhance the peach and cream tones of the existing cushions. Blue is a very traditional colour, ideally suited to the classical mood of the designs. An entirely different effect would have been achieved had the motifs been executed in bolder colours.

As can be seen on the detail overleaf, texture and depth have been added to the designs by the use of stitching around each motif. Careful application of darker colours to create areas of shadow, while highlighting others with pale or pearlized paints, also adds to the appliqued quality of the designs.

It is absolutely essential that silk paints are used when working on these covers. Ordinary fabric paints will not be absorbed into the silk cloth in the same way as silk paints are, and the fabric would, therefore, lose its delicate, shimmering quality when it is painted.

RIGHT: These beautiful cushions have been decorated by stencilling the intricate motifs onto the silk using silk paints. Areas of shadow and highlights were carefully added, using a fine artist's brush.

silk paints

SILK CUSHION COVERS

The inspiration for this series of silk cushions was wrought iron work. To create your own design, you can draw sketches or take rubbings of actual wrought iron and simplify them.

Uncluttered patterns such as these can, of course, be hand-painted, but stencilling ensures a clean, crisp edge to the pattern, and mistakes are less likely to be made.

EQUIPMENT

silk or silk cushion covers
tailor's chalk
oiled stencil card or acetate
masking tape
cutting board
scalpel or craft knife
silk paints
clean saucers
stencil brush
selection of artist's brushes
clean cloth for ironing
iron to fix the paints

ABOVE: For extra depth and definition, the stencilled pattern can be highlighted with stitching to give a padded effect.

METHOD

1 Experiment with the images you want to use on a piece of paper the same size as the cushions. Although each cushion cover is different, they are linked by the subject matter of the design and the subtle use of colour.

2 Experiment with different colour combinations, taking into consideration the background colour of the material you will be working on and the effects that can be obtained with the brushes you are using. This is time well spent before embarking on the project itself.

3 Once you are happy with your design, use tailor's chalk to mark on the cushions where the stencils will go.

4 Transfer your design onto oiled stencil card or acetate. If you use stencil card, you will have to draw the design onto the card prior to cutting it as it is not opaque. Acetate is transparent, so designs can be transferred directly onto it.

5 Fix the stencil firmly onto a cutting surface using tape. A glass surface ensures a clean edge, but tape the edges of glass to avoid accidents. A wooden cutting board can also be used.

6 Cut the pattern out of the stencil card using a craft knife or scalpel.

7 Prepare your paints, making sure that they are close to hand to avoid any drips on the material. Make sure that you have lots of clean rags available too.

8 Dip the brush into the paint. Dab it up and down evenly onto the cushion through the cut parts of the stencil using a rocking motion. Start at the edges of the stencil and work to the middle until all the spaces have been filled in.

9 Leave the fabric to dry for a few minutes with the stencil still in place. You may want to shade areas of the cushion, in which case the paint should be used at full strength.

10 Fix the colour by ironing, placing a clean cloth between the fabric and the iron.

TIPS

o *Do not overload the brush as this will cause the paint to bleed around the stencil.*

o *Always keep your designs simple — they will be much more successful when worked in one colour.*

o *Pearlized paints can be used to highlight areas of the pattern. Use fine sable brushes for highlighting.*

EMBROIDERED PICTURES

Painted abstract designs can be combined with embroidery to add contrasting colours and textures. In these pictures the water-colour effect of the silk paint is enhanced by the brightly coloured embroidery threads. The stitching is quite randomly placed using bold, traditional stitches in a very simplistic way to create more shapes and colours. The thread takes the place of a paint brush, adding bright or pale colours in small amounts, or outlines to a darker background.

Leaving the edges of the fabric frayed gives an attractive 'raw' look to the finished work. Alternatively, the edges can be stitched in a harmonizing or contrasting colour.

BELOW: Susan Kennewell's pictures illustrate how silk paints can be used on cotton to give a clearer, brighter effect than that which could be obtained with fabric paints.

mixed media

EQUIPMENT

mediumweight cotton
silk paints
masking tape
selection of artist's brushes
saucers
solvent
clean cloth for ironing
iron
embroidery thread

METHOD

1 Stretch out the fabric on a clean working surface and secure it in place down with masking tape.

2 Mix a selection of bright colours in your saucers. If you wish to use paler colours, dilute the paints to create lighter tones and shades.

3 Using a selection of brushes to create different thicknesses, paint the colours onto the fabric in stripes, merging one colour into another, adding dashes of other colours as a contrast. Although this is a random design the brushes must be washed between each colour to keep them vivid. If the brush is not kept clean, the end result will be murky. Leave the picture to dry.

4 Fix the paints by ironing, placing a piece of fabric between the design and the iron. Even though the painting is to be framed, strong light may fade the colours.

5 Embroider the picture as you wish. Before starting, lay the threads across the painted background so that the most compatible colour range is chosen.

> ### TIPS
> o *If the paint appears to be drying with hard edge, use a compatible silk paint solvent to ensure that it flows smoothly on the fabric.*

RIGHT and BELOW: Watery silk paints have been used to create these soft, merging shapes, highlighted by the use of simple embroidery stitches in contrasting colours.

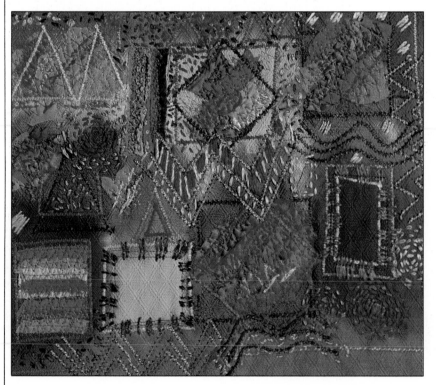

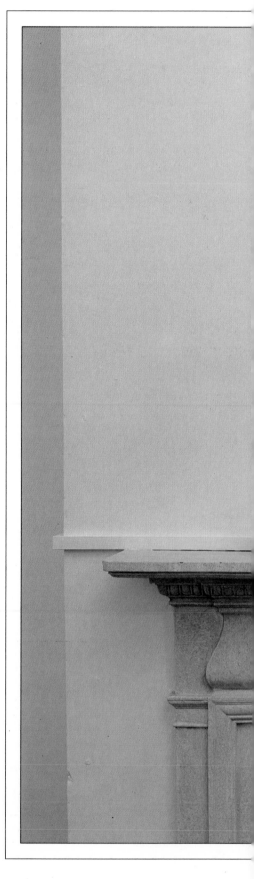

gutta

FINE ART
WALL HANGING

Although a wall hanging will not serve any practical purpose in our homes today, it will add a luxurious sense of texture and richness to the decor. It can also be a very satisfying project to design and make.

Hangings can be made out of a huge variety of fabrics, from delicate silks to heavy canvas, and painting techniques and designs are limitless. The paint itself can be combined with the use of other decorative techniques, such as embroidery, to emphasize colour and design. A mixture of fabrics and textures can often produce startling effects.

Give some thought to the way that you are going to display your work. There are many ways to do this, including the use of battens glued to the top and bottom of the hanging, stretching the cloth over a suitably sized frame, or fixing it onto a painted board leaving the edges of the board bare.

This silk wall hanging has a distinct fine art influence. Inspired by modern paintings, the brilliant colours and strong geometric shapes are all the more effective when emphasized with the gutta outline. The gutta acts as a barrier between the paint and the cloth, retaining the original colour of the fabric as a distinct border between the painted shapes.

RIGHT: The gutta outline used for this wall hanging by Claudine Dungen, retains the pale background colour of the fabric, highlighting the jewel-like paints and unusual imagery. The design has been inspired by modern artists —an infinite source of ideas for many types of fabric painting.

EQUIPMENT

white silk crepe de chine
paper
soft pencil
masking tape
gutta (percha)
silk paints
clean plates and saucers
selection of soft artist's brushes
clean cloth for ironing
iron for fixing the paint

TIPS

o *Stretch the silk as taut as possible before painting, as it will slip quite easily.*

METHOD

1 Work out your design, planning where you want the colours to fall on the hanging.

2 Using a soft pencil, draw the design to scale onto an appropriately-sized piece of paper.

3 Place the fabric over the paper, securing it in place with masking tape. You will be able to see the outline of your design quite clearly through the smooth silk.

4 Trace the design onto the fabric using a light pencil. Make sure that you do not snag the material.

5 Using the gutta in its applicator, trace the pencil lines on the cloth with the gutta. Leave it to dry thoroughly.

6 Mix your colours in separate dishes, ensuring that you have enough paint for each area.

7 Starting with the palest colours first, fill in each fabric section using a soft brush so that the silk paints flow smoothly. Wash the brush between each colour, making sure that excess moisture is squeezed out before reloading the brush with paint. This ensures that the paints do not get diluted. Leave the hanging flat to dry.

8 Fix the silk paints in place by ironing onto the fabric with a medium hot iron, placing a cloth between the fabric and the iron.

9 Wash the fabric in cool water to remove the gutta. The outline will be retained on the material.

10 Dry the silk away from direct heat or sunlight and iron with a warm iron to remove any creases.

batik | SCATTER CUSHIONS

Batik is one of the oldest forms of fabric decoration. It is the ancient art of wax-resist dyeing where hot wax is applied to the fabric to act as a block against the colour. When the fabric is immersed in dye, the wax will protect the underlying surface of the cloth, so that when the wax is removed it will leave a pattern showing the natural colour of the cloth.

India, Persia, China, Japan and Africa are noted for their wonderful Batik work. Tjanting tools, originally from the East, are used for applying wax to fabric. A tjanting is a small metal cup with a spout which is attached to a wooden handle. This ensures that the line of wax is controlled.

Batik is recognized by its veined, cracked effect which produces a unique quality which cannot be obtained by using any other method. The effect is always different and original—no two pieces can be duplicated.

The best fabrics to use for this technique are muslins and 100% cottons. The smooth surface of the cloth accepts dye well. It is best to avoid synthetic materials and very heavy coarse fabrics are not recommended.

If you do not want to use a tjanting, or have difficulty in purchasing one, brushes can be used to achieve a variety of effects and they will cover larger areas. However, it is best to use old or cheap household brushes as once used they will be ruined, losing their stiffness in the hot wax.

The best dyes to use for batik are cold water dyes. Hot dyes will melt the wax. Follow the maker's instructions closely. It is always best to use a container for dyeing which is large enough for the fabric to be totally immersed in water or uneven dying will result. If you are working on a very large fabric, a sink or bath can be used. However, you must clean the sink or bath immediately afterwards with a strong household cleaner.

The wax is removed from the cloth by placing the fabric between layers of newspaper and ironing it. This process will have to be repeated with several sheets of paper until all the wax is removed. This is a very time-consuming and messy process, but well worth the effort.

These cushions vividly portray the unique veined, cracked effect which can be produced with batik. For the best result, dye the fabric before making it into cushions, rather than using ready-made cushions. The fabric can be cut into the desired cushion size, or dyed as one piece of fabric.

ABOVE: A tjanting should be used to apply hot wax to the fabric. It will ensure a controlled line of wax, which cannot be achieved when a brush is used.

BELOW: These samplers show a variety of different ways of applying wax to fabric for striking effects. Pineapple images have been drawn onto the fabric and colour hand-painted onto different areas of the design for a fresh, bright image. The other sampler shows stripes, spots and blobs of wax applied to the fabric, which has then been over-painted with dyes and decorated with fabric crayons. When the wax is removed, these areas will show the clear patterns of the fabric base colour.

EQUIPMENT

white cotton fabric
protective paper or cloth
masking tape
pencil
batik wax
saucepan and smaller bowl or wax
    heater
tjanting or household brushes
cold water dye and manufacturer's
    recommended fixing agent
large container for dye
wooden spoon or stick
rubber gloves
lots of newspaper
iron to remove the wax

METHOD

1 Protect your working surface with paper or cloth as some wax might pass through the fabric. Stretch out the fabric over the working surface. Fasten down the edges with masking tape.

2 If you wish, guidelines showing where you want the wax to fall, can be lightly drawn in pencil onto the fabric.

3 Heat up the batik wax from a solid form into a hot liquid. This can be done by placing the wax in a bowl which is then placed in a saucepan of boiling water. Do not cover the saucepan with a lid. A much quicker way of heating the wax is by using a wax heater specially designed for this purpose.

4 Dip the tjanting or household brush into the hot wax. If the nozzle of the tjanting is blocked from a previous job, it will unblock as soon as it is dipped into the hot wax. Apply the wax directly to the fabric, using the tjanting. Lines, spots and splashes can easily be achieved using this method.

5 For a cracked effect, firmly scrunch up the material once the wax has dried. The wax will dry within seconds of being applied to the fabric.

6 Mix your dye in a large container following the manufacturer's instructions carefully. Remember to add the fixing agent to make the dye permanent. Immerse the cushions in the dye, stirring the fabric at regular intervals with a wooden spoon or stick. It is a good idea to wear rubber gloves during this process, as the dye is difficult to remove from the skin. Leave the fabric immersed in the dye solution for the recommended length of time. Stir at regular intervals to ensure that the dye penetrates all areas of the fabric.

7 When the recommended time is over, rinse the cushions thoroughly until the water runs clear

8 Once dyed, stretch the cushion covers out on a flat surface to dry.

9 Heat your iron to its hottest setting. Cover the surface of the ironing board with a thick layer of newspaper. Place more newspaper on top of fabric so that the fabric is sandwiched between the newspaper. Apply the hot iron to the paper so that the heat melts the wax and it is absorbed into the paper. This process must be repeated many times until all the wax has been removed from the fabric. The colour is now permanent and can be hand-washed or dry cleaned.

TIPS

o *An alternative to the usual method of cold water dyeing is to paint the surface of the fabric using a household brush. Use sweeping movements across the fabric for a soft watery effect.*

ABOVE: The vivid blue dye of these cushions clearly portrays the characteristic veining produced by wax drawing.

PARCHMENT WALL HANGING

Wall hangings, like paintings, can be inspired by just about anything. This one is reminiscent of old, faded and peeling parchment—an artistic reminder of something that was once decorative in itself. The colours have been carefully mixed to be compatible with the imagery, using unconventional methods to achieve the desired result. The effect is highly original and the method of execution unusual.

To achieve the old, abandoned look, a variety of techniques and fabric paints must be used, trying to give the impression of layers of wall-paper being peeled away, only to find more interesting images underneath.

Before attempting an image like this, it would be a good idea to experiment using different techniques and colours until you achieve the desired effect.

RIGHT: This unique piece of art by Steven Pettengell, demonstrates the unusual effects that can be achieved by experimenting with different techniques and paints which have been applied to the surface of the canvas in layers.

EQUIPMENT

canvas
lino
soft pencil
lino cutting tools
masking tape
multi-purpose fabric paints
clean containers
old toothbrush or atomizer
natural sponge
piece of glass
roller
fabric crayons
kitchen scourer or steel wool
black fabric felt pen
clean cloth for ironing
iron to fix the paints

TIPS

o *Remember that you are creating a unique piece of art. All pieces of hand-painted fabric are different and unrepeatable, so don't worry if you think you have made a mistake on this project. The image can be altered by scraping away the paint or adding new textures.*

o *This type of wall hanging is best displayed when stretched tautly around a wooden frame.*

METHOD

1 Carefully draw the main design you are going to use onto a lino block using a pencil. Gouge the floral pattern out of the lino using the appropriate cutting tool.

2 Stretch out the canvas over your working surface and secure it firmly down with masking tape.

3 Mix the paints you are going to use in clean containers. Pale, dull tones with white added to the colours will give the desired effect.

4 Start by spraying grey and patches of cream over the canvas using either an old toothbrush or an atomizer. Leave to dry.

5 Use a natural sponge to dab colour and washes of grey over the fabric. Leave to dry.

6 Pour out a small amount of fabric paint onto a piece of glass. Spread it out evenly with a roller. Using the roller, cover the lino cut evenly with paint.

7 Using the lino, print brown floral shapes in patches over the canvas. Leave to dry.

8 Use fabric crayons over the top of the paints. Leave to dry.

9 Continue layering the crayons and paints over each other, leaving each layer to dry, until the paint is thick and textured. You do not have to have exactly the same thickness of paint in each area because this hanging relies on its unusual textured design.

10 Using a kitchen scourer or piece of wire wool, scratch through the layers in patches, exposing the different paint finishes. This will give a rough texture as well as creating the flaky, ancient imagery.

11 Using a black felt pen, draw or doodle in the scrubbed areas. This will convey an image of ancient manuscripts and papers.

12 Allow the hanging to dry thoroughly.

13 Fix by ironing, placing a piece of fabric between the wall hanging and the iron and iron evenly over the surface of the fabric.

The attractive colouring and design of the Willow pattern
has been used to enhance the blue and white china tea set
with a co-ordinating tea cosy design.

EATING

A plain kitchen or dining area can be transformed by the ingenious use of decorated fabric accessories. Whether your eating area is starkly modern or warmly traditional in style, you can let your imagination run riot and create a whole host of items to brighten up this essentially functional area. Tablecloths, napkins, placemats, oven gloves, and blinds are just a few of the things you can decorate to add a new dimension to the kitchen.

Table linen can contribute to the atmosphere of a meal — it can be romantic and pretty for intimate dining, elegant for formal dinner parties, bright and cheerful for everyday use, or fun and adventurous for children. However, when deciding on your design, the overall decor of the room and the existing tableware should be taken into account.

Design ideas can be culled from a wide variety of sources. A detail from an attractive dinner service can be picked out and utilized, for example, an unusual colour combination or motif could form the basis of a design.

Elements from nature are another possible source of inspiration. Fruits and vegetables — grapes, mangoes, pineapples — with their glorious shapes and colours provide limitless design ideas. Even a humble bunch of onions or garlic can be used to emphasize the atmosphere of a rustic country kitchen. The vegetables and fruits themselves, for instance, carrots and potatoes, can be used cut, or uncut, to make exciting textured prints on kitchen items.

When selecting fabrics to be used in the kitchen, bear in mind the frequent washing that they will need. Hardwearing fabrics such as linen or cotton should, therefore, be used. These particular fabrics have the added advantage of being ideal for fabric painting, although care must be taken to remove any manufacturer's finish which will prevent the paints from being evenly absorbed into the material.

Man made materials, for instance PVC (plastic-coated fabrics), are also useful in the kitchen. Easy to clean, and ideal for households with children, plastic-coated fabrics can be used for tablecloths, placemats, window blinds or for lining drawers and shelves. Plastic paints can be used to create original, exciting effects. As these paints are not absorbed into the material, the colours remain vivid, forming a raised, textured surface on the fabric.

It is particularly important to ensure that the paints you use are made permanent. Not only will items need frequent washing, but they will also be exposed to steam. It is, therefore, just as important to ensure that the colours in a kitchen wall hanging are made permanent, as it is to carefully fix the paint used on tea towels.

WILLOW-PATTERNED TEA COSY

Blue and white tableware, particularly when it conjures up images of the Far East, has been a classic in our homes for many generations. The quality of colour and the style of design for the tea cosy shown overleaf were based on the ancient Willow pattern, using blue fabric paints on white cotton. The inspiration for the design was an old Willow-pattern plate.

Although it may be possible to buy a ready-made, plain tea cosy to paint, the best results will be achieved if the design is worked onto fabric before making up. Choose a light or medium-weight cotton, remembering that you will also need lining and padding for the tea cosy.

It is essential to work out the design for the tea cosy in detail, considering its shape and dimensions. A simple paper pattern can be cut out and used, sketching the design to its actual size.

To achieve the varied range of blue tones, silk paints were used, adding water to give lighter tones. The gutta acts as a blocker to prevent the paints bleeding into the fabric.

EQUIPMENT

fabric for tea cosy
pencil
paper
medium-weight cotton
masking tape
silk paints
clean saucers
gutta (percha)
selection of fine artist's brushes
clean cloth for ironing
iron to fix the paints

METHOD

1 Prepare the design in sketch form, finalizing the basic plan for the arrangement of the design on the tea cosy.

2 Cut the fabric for the tea cosy, allowing enough material for the seams. Stretch it out on your working surface and secure the pieces down with masking tape.

3 Mix the paints in clean saucers, blending a full range of blue tones, from very pale blue to an intense, dark blue.

4 Trace the lines of the design onto the fabric with gutta, remembering that where the line of blocker is drawn no colour will penetrate. Allow the gutta to dry completely.

5 Apply the paints carefully, using a fine artist's brush. Light shades of colour should be applied first. It is difficult to lighten an area once a dark paint has been applied, so start with light tones and increase the density of the colour. Allow the paints to dry completely.

6 Make a final check of the design to ensure that it is well-balanced, with the right amount of colour and detail. At this stage more colour can be added.

7 Fix the colour by ironing the fabric on a high temperature setting for several minutes on the reverse side of the fabric.

8 Wash the fabric in warm, soapy water, allowing it to soak for about five minutes. The line of gutta will begin to disappear, revealing the design more clearly. If some of the blocker does not soak away, give the fabric a gentle rub to assist in removing the gutta from the fabric fibres. Leave the fabric to dry. Once ironed, it is ready to be made into the tea cosy.

TIPS

o *Some of the gutta may seep through the material onto the paper protecting your working surface, especially if a fine fabric is used. If you are using paper to protect your work surface, bits of it may stick to the fabric. This will easily come away when the fabric is soaked in soapy water.*

o *Once the tea cosy is made, accompanying design features can be added, for example a tablecloth or napkins, each following the above instructions.*

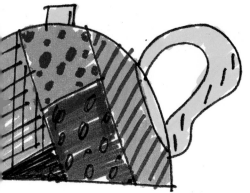

LEFT: Design ideas and experiments using a variety of colours and design styles, were worked through before tackling the actual project.

stencilling

FRUITY TEA TOWELS

Colour and decoration can be added to kitchens by adding imaginative, home spun details. A tea cosy, oven gloves and tea towels can all be given a personal touch by adding a border design or by using an all-over pattern. Simple motifs which relate to the room, such as painted fruit, vegetables, leaves and kitchen utensils are all fun themes to experiment with.

EQUIPMENT

white cotton tea towels
paper
pencil
stencil acetate
scalpel or craft knife
fabric paints
saucers for mixing
graph paper
glass surface for cutting
masking tape
stencil brush
clean cloth for ironing
iron for fixing paints

METHOD

1 Draw a simple pear shape and an apple shape to scale on paper. Alternatively, cut an apple and a pear in half and draw around them using a pencil. Add a leaf and a stalk to each fruit shape.

2 Work out how many motifs will be used across each tea towel. To ensure that the fruits are equally spaced, draw a row of apples and a row of pears to scale on paper. Although more time will be spent making the stencil, a great deal of time will be saved when making sure that the positioning of the motifs is accurate. Graph paper will assist in lining up the motifs.

3 Lay the stencil acetate over the drawn fruit and, using a sharp knife, cut out the stencils. You will have two rows of stencils—one of apples and one of pears. A smoother edge will be achieved if the stencil is cut on a glass surface.

4 Mix the colours in clean saucers, making sure that the paint is not too thin. If it is too runny, it may seep under the edge of the stencil.

5 Stretch out the tea towels over your working surface and secure them down with masking tape. Lay the stencil in position over the top of the tea towel. Secure it down with masking tape.

6 Dipping a stencil brush lightly in the fabric paint, fill in the stencil shapes. The motifs have a textured appearance which is achieved by using dabbing strokes with the brush. Allow the paint to dry before removing the stencil.

7 Repeat the motifs, remembering to wash and dry the brush before changing colour. When finished, leave the tea towels to dry on a flat surface.

8 Cover each towel with a clean cloth and fix the paints by ironing evenly over the surface for several minutes using a hot iron.

TIPS
o *Keep the stencil brush very dry. This will ensure a sharper edge and a more interesting texture.*

ABOVE: Carrots, mushrooms and cut potatoes have been dipped into fabric paint and firmly pressed onto the fabric to print these unusual samples.

LEFT: These simple border designs have been created by using stencils cut in the stylized shapes of apples and pears.

acrylic paints

FLOORCLOTH

Floorcloths are an attractive and unusual alternative to rugs. They used to be especially popular in Europe and America until 'instant' floor-coverings, such as linoleum and wall-to-wall carpets, became popular. Floorcloths look especially effective when placed over natural or painted floorboards or earthenware tiles.

Nowadays, floorcloths are made by painting over a closely woven canvas, which is then primed and varnished. This renders the material particularly hardwearing and stain-resistant. Ease of cleaning makes floorcloths an ideal covering for use in the kitchen or dining room. They can also be used in the children's playroom or the bathroom.

When painting a large floorcloth, the major problem to overcome is lack of space, as ease of access is essential when designing and working. The work may have to be executed with the cloth laid in place or, better still, in the garden or backyard where the smells of paint, primer and varnish will be dispersed. However, bear in mind that the layers of varnish must be left to dry overnight, so a favourable long-term weather forecast is essential. The warmer it is, the more quickly the varnish will dry. Stretching the canvas over a home-made wooden frame will enable you to move the floorcloth with ease while it is still wet. As the floorcloth may take several days to prime, paint and varnish, a frame could prove to be very useful if space is limited. The frame should be made out of a light-weight wood, so that it is not too heavy to lift.

The scope for design is endless—sponging, spraying, spattering, block-printing, lino cuts and stencilling are all possibilities. The design can be bold and bright or soft and subtle, according to your existing decor. Old floor tiles or marble are ideal sources of inspiration, especially those of Middle Eastern or Mediterranean origin. Look through travel guides, old books, museums and galleries for ideas.

BELOW: This canvas painted by Jona Carlyon, has been decorated with acrylic paints creating a hard-wearing floorcloth that is also a unique work of art. This type of imagery is more usually associated with a painting hung on the wall, but looks just as effective when used on the floor.

EQUIPMENT

closely woven thick canvas
frame to work on (optional)
primer
sandpaper
assortment of brushes, including a
 very large brush for applying the
 primer and a large varnishing brush
acrylic paints
clean containers for blending the
 paints
varnish
white spirit or turpentine
 (to dilute the varnish)
strong glue

METHOD

1 Cut the canvas to the required size, remembering to allow enough material around the edges for the hem.

2 Prime the canvas using a product specially manufactured for this purpose. It will protect the fabric from wear and tear and provide an even surface for painting on. At least five coats of primer will be necessary. It should be brushed on evenly, right up to the edges, and allowed to dry thoroughly between each application.

3 Sand each layer of primer down after the third layer has been applied. This will make the surface of the floorcloth smooth.

4 Apply three coats of primer to the back of the canvas to protect it. Again, allow each layer to dry before applying the next.

5 The geese have been painted onto the canvas using freestyle brush strokes. While this technique is, in itself, quite easy, there may be difficulty in capturing the realistic quality of the geese. To make this easier, use a photograph or painting as a guideline. Grids can be drawn over a picture and then enlarged, square by square onto the canvas. Alternatively, if you have access to a projector, a transparency can be projected onto the canvas and the images traced using a pencil.

6 Prepare your paints. Acrylic paints give a good density of colour. Make sure that you have blended enough paints to finish the floorcloth as it may be difficult to match the colours.

7 Apply the paints to the canvas using a selection of brushes for outlining and detailing. All the colours are rich and are painted so that they blend in with each other. Remember that even if the imagery has been difficult to capture on the canvas, imaginative use of colours will create a beautiful result. Leave the canvas to dry.

8 Apply the varnish. About four coats will be necessary to provide the desired protection. The first two coats of varnish should be diluted with white spirit. Each application of varnish should be done as quickly and thinly as possible and left to dry overnight. Apply a coat of varnish to the back of the canvas to protect it.

9 Once the floorcloth has dried thoroughly, turn the edges under and glue them down.

TIPS

o *Using a frame will produce a better end result. It can be easily made at home by nailing together four light pieces of wood. The canvas can be stretched over it and pinned down, keeping it very taut. This will produce much better results when painting and will make it easier to apply the primer and varnish. Also, the floorcloth can be moved without too much difficulty while it is wet.*

o *Treat the floorcloth as if it were a painting. If you are not happy with certain areas of the design, leave it to dry and then repaint it. The paint underneath will not show through.*

o *Do not apply the coats of varnish too thickly. If too much varnish is used, the images on the canvas will appear darker and less vibrant.*

o *When purchasing the glue, make sure that it is a type which will not leave a stain on the canvas and that will stay flexible when dry.*

silk paints

FRACTURED WALL PIECE

Ordinary dressmaker's interfacing has been used to create this dramatic wall piece. Interfacing can be purchased at very little cost. There are a variety of weights to choose from—a medium- to heavyweight fabric was used for this project. The differing fabric thicknesses will affect the intensity of the fabric paint when applied.

The 'fractured' effect was achieved by literally peeling away layers of fabric to break up the image. The pieces can be glued or, alternatively, stitched back onto the fine base of interfacing. In this example, bright embroidery threads were used, incorporating them into the design.

Any variety of paint ideas can be employed to create the desired image. Sample pieces of fabric should be tried out first before tackling the main project to check the intensity of the paint on the fabric.

EQUIPMENT

medium- to heavyweight fabric
    interfacing
paper or cloth to protect your work
    surface
silk paints
fabric inks
clean saucers
artist's brushes
pencil
clean cloth to protect the ironing
    board and iron
iron to fix the paints
multi-purpose glue
embroidery threads and needle
painted board for mounting
    (optional)

METHOD

1 Protect your working surface with paper or cloth as the paint will seep through the fabric onto your work table. Secure the fabric down with masking tape.

2 Mix the colours, following the results of your experiments on sample pieces of interfacing. Silk dyes and coloured inks were used for this design. They were encouraged to bleed into each other with the application of water.

3 Apply the paints to your fabric using a selection of artist's brushes. The designs which can be created are unlimited. If you wish, light marks can be made on the fabric beforehand, using a pencil to indicate design layout.

4 Once the fabric has dried, fix the paints by ironing. Cover both the ironing board and the fabric with thin paper or cloth to prevent staining.

5 To create the fractured image, separate the layers of interfacing, peeling them away from the base layer. Irregular shapes will occur, making this a spontaneous design.

6 Position the pieces and fragments of interfacing onto the thin piece of interfacing that is left. This can be very effective if some of the shapes are replaced just a little away from their original positions. Other pieces of fabric can be turned upside down.

7 When you are happy with the image, glue the pieces of fabric into place or, alternatively, coloured threads can be used to attach them to the base layer of fabric.

TIPS

o *The threads can blend with the paint colours or clash and contrast. Elaborate embroidery stitches can be used to highlight certain areas of the wall piece.*

o *This wall piece can be displayed in a variety of ways. In this case, it was mounted on a white painted board.*

RIGHT: The strong, rich colours of this wall piece are dramatically enhanced by the stark, white-washed brick of the kitchen wall.

PEACH TABLECLOTH

Plain tablecloths which have become faded or dowdy can be revamped and given a new lease of life with the imaginative use of fabric paints. This ready-made tablecloth was decorated with repeated images using very basic stencil shapes and simple potato prints.

The triangles and squares were stencilled directly onto the cloth and the smaller squares and oblongs were created from potato shapes which were cut and printed onto the cloth.

If the tablecloth you are working on is very large, it may be easier to prepare a work area on the floor. This will allow access all around the cloth and allows you to assess how the pattern is developing as you work.

EQUIPMENT

cotton tablecloth
paper and pencil
masking tape
clean saucers
thick cardboard
craft knife
potatoes
sponge or stencil brush
iron

METHOD

1 Prepare your design on paper, experimenting with very basic potato print effects and simple stencils. Ensure that the colours you are going to use are appropriate to the design.

2 Secure the cloth down onto the working surface, using masking tape.

3 Prepare the fabric paints in clean saucers, blending the colours that you wish to use. Make sure that you have mixed enough paint to complete the project.

4 Cut the stencils out of thick cardboard using a craft knife. It will be easier to move the stencil if it is fairly large. Prepare the potato shapes. For a less watery finish, allow the potato to dry out for 30 minutes before printing.

5 Work the shapes in a methodical way around the border of the fabric. The stencilled shapes can be filled in with a sponge or stencil brush, dabbing the paint onto the fabric. Make sure that you do not smear the paint when removing the stencil. Wash the brush or sponge before changing colour. The scattered shapes in the centre of the cloth are randomly positioned. Let the border dry before painting the centre of the cloth to avoid smearing the paint. Once you are happy with your design, leave the cloth to dry overnight.

6 Fix the paints by ironing onto the reverse side of the fabric with a hot iron.

TIPS

o *The tablecloth may be rather stiff after painting. To soften it, wash the fabric in warm soap suds after the colours have been made permanent.*

LEFT: *This tablecloth has been decorated using sponges and cut potatoes dipped into fabric dye. The soft background colour creates a warm, fresh look.*

CHIAROSCURO NAPKINS

Table linen has both a practical and a decorative purpose. Although it is no longer considered to be an essential item in the kitchen or dining room, a hand-painted tablecloth with matching napkins still adds a luxurious and individual touch to special occasion settings.

Painting a tablecloth may seem a daunting project, but decorating a set of napkins is easily manageable. As the area is fairly small, an intricate design can be used that may not be practical on a larger area.

A quick but very effective way of adding individuality to napkins is to decorate each corner with a motif. A simple finishing touch, such as a plain border can be used, painting each napkin in a different colour. This type of design is particularly attractive when displayed on a white tablecloth.

Design inspiration may be found in an attractive dinner service, or you may wish to decorate for a special occasion such as Chirstmas, a birthday or a wedding party. Names or traditional symbols, such as wedding bells, Christmas trees and snowmen, can be utilized.

Napkins can be made, using cotton or linen fabric, but it is much quicker and easier to use bought ones. If you do decide to make your own napkins, they should be painted *before* they are hemmed.

The crisp design on the napkins shown overleaf, echoes the black and white pattern on the cups and saucers and the vase.

Simplified duck shapes have been cut out of lino to give a naive print style. Additional textural effects are achieved when printing on varied fabrics.

lino cuts

EQUIPMENT

cotton napkins
paper
pencil
masking tape
thick linoleum
lino cutting tools
fabric paint
clean saucers
glass
roller
clean cloth for ironing
iron to fix the paints

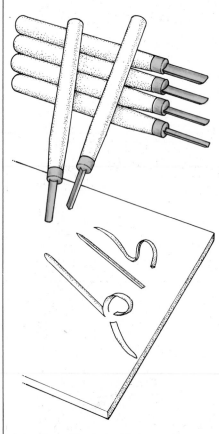

ABOVE: Lino cutting tools will give varying thicknesses of line and depth for your lino prints.

METHOD

1 Experiment with design ideas, making rough sketches on paper until you have finalized your design. For these napkins two separate design blocks were used.

2 Stretch the napkins out onto your work surface and secure the edges with masking tape. You may want to print one at a time or, if space allows, they can be printed simultaneously.

3 Cut two appropriately sized pieces of linoleum. Don't cut the lino too small or it will be difficult to press it onto the fabric. Copy your final design, using a pencil, onto the lino. Gouge the design out of the lino following the pencilled guidelines. Different cutting tools are used for different thicknesses of line.

4 Pour a small amount of fabric paint onto the piece of glass. Carefully spread the paint out over the glass using the roller until the roller is evenly covered with a thin layer of paint.

5 Using the roller, cover the two pieces of lino evenly with fabric paint. Apply the paint very sparingly. If too much paint is used, the textures of the pattern will disappear when you are printing.

6 Turn the lino face down onto the fabric, applying firm and even pressure. Carefully remove the lino. The print should be quite textured and rather reminiscent of an etching or engraving.

7 Repeat the prints over the fabric. It is not necessary to repaint the lino for each print. Allow plenty of space between the motifs so that they do not overlap. It is all too easy to print the motifs too close to one another, thereby spoiling the overall appearance of the design.

8 Once the paint has dried, fix the dye in place by ironing onto the painted side of the fabric with a hot iron, placing a cloth between the fabric and the iron.

TIPS

o *To avoid accidents, cover the edges of the glass with a thick layer of masking tape.*

o *If a roller is not available, a brush can be used instead. Ensure that the paint is applied evenly.*

o *If you wish to use more than one colour on the napkins, wash and dry the lino carefully before changing colours. Remember to remove excess paint from the grooves as this could spoil the clarity of the next colour you are going to use.*

RIGHT: The crisp black and white of the tableware is vividly accentuated by the yellow roses. This bold colour combination gives a 1950s flavour to the setting.

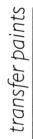

KITCHEN FLOWERS

The inspiration for this design was taken from a jug of flowers. Their fresh, bright appeal makes a lovely decoration on the kitchen wall. The image was drawn quite freely from the actual jug of flowers with little attention being given to detail. The desired effect was simply to show a jug full of fresh flower shapes.

The transfer colours were used without blending or mixing them. They were diluted with water to make the paler shades. The transparent quality of the colour, especially when worked on a satin fabric, produces a very pleasing effect. A variety of different fabrics can be used for transfer printing, but the best results are achieved on 100% polyester fabrics.

EQUIPMENT
polyester fabric
protective paper
watercolour paints for preliminary
   sketches
selection of artist's brushes
newsprint
masking tape
transfer paints
clean cloth to protect the ironing
   board
iron to transfer the image onto
   the fabric

LEFT: This fresh, brightly coloured transfer image adds charm and character to its rustic setting. Weaving the newsprint, as shown above, will add a textured effect to the print.

METHOD

1 Cover your work surface with protective paper and ensure that all your utensils are close to hand.

2 Prepare preliminary sketches of your design ideas. Use ordinary watercolour paints on paper to achieve a similar effect. This will help you to finalize your ideas as well as giving you confidence to use the transfer paints directly onto the fabric.

3 Lay the newsprint onto the work surface and secure the corners down with masking tape. There is no need to tape all the outer edges.

4 Prepare your paints, diluting them with water if you want a softer shade.

5 Apply one colour at a time to the newsprint. The colours will dry very quickly. If you apply a new coat of colour onto a wet one the colour will bleed. The image will look flat and dry on paper, but will alter completely once it has been transferred onto the fabric.

6 Cover your ironing board with a protective cloth to prevent any staining. Lay the polyester fabric over the protective cloth, then lay the paper design face down onto the fabric.

7 Iron the fabric slowly and evenly over the design area with a hot iron, taking care not to scorch the material.

8 Check the colour by peeling up one corner of the paper. If the colour transferred onto the fabric is still rather pale, more heat is needed. Do not remove your paper image from contact with the fabric until you are satisfied with the colour penetration. Once the design has been removed, it is very difficult to place back in exactly the same position on the fabric.

9 Once the colour is bright enough, your transfer image is ready for hanging. Extra effects can be achieved by stitching or embroidery. The use of padding can give you an unusual cushioned effect. Texture can be added by using transfer crayons.

TIPS
o *Before you start on the main piece, it is a good idea to test the colours you are going to use by transferring them onto a small sample piece of fabric. This will also enable you to ensure that your iron is set at the correct temperature — if it is too cool the colours will be pale and if it is too hot, the fabric will melt.*

BERRY NAPKINS

Inspired by a traditional piece of hand embroidery, the delicate pattern on these napkins is fairly time-consuming to reproduce, but the lovely results are well worth the effort.

The leaves and berries were traced from the original piece of embroidery, and then expanded to fit within the area of the napkins.

EQUIPMENT

cotton napkins
paper
pencil
fabric paints
clean saucers
stencil acetate
masking tape
craft knife
selection of artist's brushes, including
    a stencil brush
clean cloth for ironing
iron to fix the paints

METHOD

1 Cut out a piece of paper to exactly the same size as your napkins and draw the design that you wish to use onto it to scale.

2 Mix the paint colours in clean saucers. The vivid red for the berries can be used straight from the pot, but do not overload the brush.

3 Cut out a piece of stencil acetate slightly bigger than the size of the napkin and place the acetate over the top of the paper design, smoothing out any wrinkles or irregularities in either surface. Use masking tape to keep it in place.

4 Using the craft knife, carefully cut all the leaf motifs out of the stencil acetate. This is quite an intricate design—take care that you do not tear the stencil while cutting it. The berries can be hand-painted on the napkins afterwards.

5 Stretch out as many napkins as you are going to use on a flat surface, fixing them firmly down with masking tape. It is much quicker to stencil the napkins one after the other. Place the stencil acetate over each napkin, fixing it firmly down with masking tape.

6 Paint the leaves through the stencil onto the napkin using a dabbing motion. Make sure that you position the stencil in the same place over the napkin each time. As the leaves are painted using more than one shade, it is impossible to produce identical napkins, but this adds to the individuality and charm of the finished result.

7 After the leaves have been allowed to dry, paint in the berries using a very small amount of fabric paint on a fine brush.

8 Once the fabric has dried, fix the dye in place by ironing on the painted side of the fabric with a hot iron, placing a cloth between the fabric and the iron.

TIPS

o *Wipe the acetate between stencilling each napkin to remove any excess paint.*

o *Ensure that the masking tape does not cover areas of the napkin that you wish to paint, as a gap of unpainted material will be left on the fabric.*

RIGHT AND BELOW: Delicately painted and stencilled leaves and berries are a charming addition to a festive table setting.

TURQUOISE TABLE NAPKINS

These white cotton napkins have been transformed using a new, 'high-tech' version of the old traditional tie dyeing technique—microwave dyeing. The method is much quicker and just as effective as the traditional one, but the size of the items to be dyed is limited by the size of your microwave. However, it is quick and easy and great fun, and can be used to transform lots of smaller household items such as pillowcases, napkins, tea towels, or cushion covers.

This method can be used on cotton, polyester/cotton, linen and silk, but is not suitable for woollens or synthetic fabrics. Remember that nothing with metal such as studs or zips can be put into the microwave.

BELOW: A vivid turquoise dye was selected for these white cotton napkins to create a fresh, summery atmosphere.

EQUIPMENT

white cotton napkins
rubber gloves
bowl suitable for use in a microwave
    —ensure that there is enough
    room for the turntable to rotate
natural fabric dye
plastic bag
plastic spoon to stir the dye
microwave oven

METHOD

1 Wash the napkins thoroughly in warm, soapy water to remove any special finishes. If you want a strong, defined pattern, let them dry completely before knotting or twisting them to create the patterns. If you want a more subtle effect, leave the fabric damp.

2 Prepare the napkins to create the desired pattern. **Scrunching** the fabric into a small ball will give a subtle shaded result, almost like marbling, with the colour ranging from very pale to very intense. **Knotting** the fabric into one or several knots will give circular patterns. Remember that the tighter you tie the knots the more distinct the pattern will be. **Twisting** the fabric will give a wave-like pattern, but remember to hold the twist in place when you start rinsing, or the dye will run into the patterns you have just created. **Folding** or pleating the fabric will give sharp, geometric patterns, leaving white areas along the folds.

3 Wearing rubber gloves, carefully tap the dye into the bowl and gradually stir in the amount of water recommended by the manufacturer. Ensure that the dye has dissolved completely.

4 Place the fabric in the bowl, swishing it around to ensure that it is thoroughly immersed in the dye.

5 Cover the bowl with a plastic bag, then place the bowl into the microwave oven. Set the microwave oven on 'HIGH' for four minutes.

6 After four minutes, remove the bowl from the oven. Remember to protect your hands from the heat.

7 Pour the dye solution out of the bowl, taking great care not to burn yourself with the steam or hot water. Do not undo any knots, twists or folds until the dye has been rinsed out of the fabric.

8 When the water is running almost clear, remove the knots, folds, etc, and wash the fabric in hot water using your normal soap powder to remove all traces of dye.

9 Dry the napkins away from direct sunlight or heat. Do not place them over a heater to dry.

TIPS

o *Remember that the tighter the knots or twists you tie, the sharper the pattern on the napkins will be.*

o *To create a two-tone effect, untie some of the knots after the first dyeing, then tie some more and re-dye in a different colour.*

o *To create a two-tone effect, place just one half of the fabric in the dye. Micro-dye for four minutes, then rinse as normal. Do the same with the other half of the fabric in a different colour. The effect will be one colour at one end, the second colour at the other end, and a blend of the two in the middle of the fabric.*

BELOW: Before immersing in dye, these napkins have been pleated and twisted to produce stunning colour effects.

TRELLISED TABLECLOTH

It is possible to create a beautifully co-ordinated and original look to your home by adding hand-painted items—a tablecloth; scatter cushions; a lampshade—to more permanent furnishings such as a sofa, curtain or even a carpet, that already have a definite pattern.

You can, of course, often buy identical or matching furnishing fabrics to those you already have, but a plethora of ready-painted fabrics can look tired and unimaginative, whereas a hand-painted item will 'lift' existing decor and be an original focal point to the room.

BELOW: Painting fabrics to co-ordinate with existing furnishings is an effective way of adding a unique touch to an otherwise formal scheme. Here, the tablecloth has been hand-painted to echo the pattern on the curtains and chair.

Remember that the charm of hand-painted fabrics is their irregularity and the fact you can use design motifs which do not repeat to a standard format. Instead, pick out design elements and colours which you find appealing, taking one small section of the existing pattern such as a leaf or a flower or something more abstract.

Although it can be easier to match the colours of your design to those of the existing fabric than to create an original colour combination, it is important to mix colours which complement your motif. Colours which work beautifully on bought material can often look too subtle or too overpowering on a hand-painted fabric because the brush strokes will be varied and textured instead of being flat areas of colour.

Experiment with your ideas on scraps of the material you are going to use until you feel that the colour and pattern are perfectly balanced. Once you have selected a design you like, place the sample next to the bought material and make sure that they work well together. Come back to the design the following day with a 'fresh eye' to make sure that it is still pleasing!

'Fabric matching' can be used throughout the home—napkins can be painted to complement a patterned tablecloth, curtains to match a quilt cover, floor rugs to echo existing wallpaper. But, whatever you create, always bear in mind that the simplest design are the most effective.

To complement the powerful pattern of the curtains, a small section of their design has been simplified and then repeated around the edge of the tablecloth, creating a very soft, fluid effect in muted tones.

TIPS

o *Don't attempt to use material which has a textured weave because you will not be able to achieve a clear outline or an even paint finish. If the fabric is new, make sure that the manufacturer's finish has been washed out. If it is not new, make sure that the article has been thoroughly cleaned.*

o *Wash out the brushes in clean water before changing colours. Squeeze out any excess water before re-loading the brush with paint.*

EQUIPMENT

cotton/polyester tablecloth
pencil
paper
masking tape
fabric paints
selection of artist's brushes
clean saucers
clean cloth for ironing
iron to fix the paints

METHOD

1 Sketch out your ideas on paper, constantly referring to the fabric you are co-ordinating it with. Experiment with stylizing and simplifying the pattern of the bought fabric. The design shown here is composed of very small section of the pattern on the curtains.

2 Once you are happy with your design, draw it to scale on a large piece of paper cut to the same size and shape as the tablecloth. This will

enable you to check that the proportions of the pattern look correct and that the size of the motifs co-ordinate with the existing fabric. The design shown here is the same on each quarter, so it is not necessary to draw out the whole tablecloth.

3 Stretch out the tablecloth on your working surface, ensuring that there are absolutely no creases. Secure it down firmly with tape. If you don't have a large enough working area, prepare one half of the tablecloth in turn, waiting for the paint to dry before starting on the other half.

4 Transfer your design onto the fabric using a soft pencil. The pencil marks will wash out. If the fabric is fairly transparent, put the paper design underneath it and trace directly onto the fabric. As this particular design is quite a flexible one, accuracy is not too important.

5 Assemble all the painting equipment onto your work area. Mix the required colours in the clean saucers. As the colours used on the tablecloth are quite subtle, start with white, blending in small amounts of paint until the right shade is achieved. Test the colours you are going to use on a scrap of fabric to ensure that it is not too subtle or too overpowering.

6 Paint the design onto the cloth, starting with the lightest colours. To prevent smudges, paint the motifs furthest away from you first. Once the design is complete, leave it to dry flat without removing the masking tape.

7 Fix the design onto the material by covering it with a perfectly clean piece of cloth and ironing it for several minutes with a hot iron. The fabric is now washable.

*Simple shapes painted in black on white shades
give a dramatic effect to lampshades which is emphasized
when the light shines through.*

SLEEPING

The decor in the bedroom deserves a great deal of thought. It is, after all, the place we escape to at the end of the day and should, therefore, offer a restful, sympathetic atmosphere.

Whether the mood you want to create is romantic or grandly opulent, fabric painting offers lots of exciting ways to create or emphasize the mood in the bedroom. Fabric can be used to a grand scale—curtains, drapes, continental quilt covers, sheets and pillowcases, bedspreads and wall hangings all offer endless opportunities.

The most obvious candidate for fabric painting is the bedlinen. Sheets which have passed their best can be made to look fresh and new with fabric dyes. A multitude of colours can be used, from gentle pastels to chic black. Because well-washed cotton is ideal for dyeing, the results will be fabulous. Sophisticated borders can be stencilled or hand-painted onto the bedlinen, or sheets can be spattered or sponged for original, exciting effects.

Tie dyeing is an inexpensive and simple way of giving the bedlinen a completely new look. With care, and a little experience, a spectacular array of effects can be created with this very traditional method of dyeing, including zebra stripes and soft marbling. Use shades of blue to give the room a restful mood, or earthy browns for a warmer appeal.

Cotton bedspreads can also be decorated, as long as the base colour is pale. You will not be able to successfully print or dye over dark materials. The texture of the fabric must also be taken into account—if it is uneven it will be unsuitable for most forms of printing, ie stencilling or block printing, although the fabric weave can sometimes be successfully incorporated into the design. Alternatively, a length of thick cotton can be decorated and used as a bedcover. It is, of course, important to remove any manufacturer's special finish, as this will prevent the fabric paints from being absorbed into the material.

Wall hangings are particularly successful in the bedroom because, unlike posters or pictures, they lend texture and depth to the surroundings. Again, the design can blend into the room, for instance a beautiful piece of tie-dyed fabric to echo the bedlinen. Alternatively, it can be a large, exotic piece of art, perhaps incorporating several paint mediums, which will add an entirely new dimension to the room. If the bedroom is large enough, a hand-painted screen can be added, as a unique focal point to the room.

Smaller, less time-consuming items, such as scatter cushions and lampshades can be cleverly used to add interest to the decor. Because such a small area of fabric is involved, they are quick and easy to work on and the designs will not overpower the room.

HAND-PAINTED LAMPSHADES

As the striking lampshades on the previous page demonstrate, a simple design can take on a dramatic appearance by limiting the use of colour to black and white. This exciting combination has been a favourite regularly used by artists throughout history, and lovely examples of monochrome work can be found in museums, art galleries and places of historical interest throughout the world. For instance, Etruscan pottery beautifully portrays the simple, but powerful effects which can be achieved with this classical colour scheme. Black and white tiling—beloved by the Romans, the Greeks and the Victorians—also creates powerful imagery which can be utilized for your own work.

In recent years, black and white design has become associated with hard, uncompromising decor, as demonstrated by 'high tech'. However, the use of curves and soft, flowing shapes, rather than rigid lines and angles, will give the design a gentle, fluid appeal. To soften the effect further, another colour can be introduced, for instance red or blue. Try out simple ideas on paper before starting the main project. This will enable you to ascertain how much colour can be added before losing the impact of the black and white.

BELOW: These sketches illustrate how various design ideas and colours were considered before painting the lampshades. The hanging shade on the right, subtly uses red to soften the hard impact of a geometric design.

EQUIPMENT

fabric lampshades
pencil
paper
tape measure
fabric paint
clean saucer
selection of artist's paint brushes
hairdryer

TIPS

o *Check to see if there are any gaps in the design by looking at the lampshade from a distance; they can be filled by adding extra motifs.*

o *Fill in any areas of black that are not evenly painted. When the light shines through the shades, the black could look patchy.*

METHOD

1 Experiment on white paper using simple black shapes. Repeat the motifs to give an indication of how the finished design will look. You may want to introduce a second colour, as shown on the sketches on page 90. The shapes should not be too large, as too much black can be over-powering on a small area.

2 Using a tape measure, work out where the motifs are going to appear on each lampshade. Mark each place with a pencil. When you are certain that the spacing will be even all the way around each shade, draw the 'wiggles' in lightly, using a pencil. Draw the guidelines for the chess-board effect. Adjust the size of the squares so that they fit evenly all the way around the shade without any gaps.

3 Pour the black fabric paint into the saucer. Although it is possible to work straight from the pot, pouring the paint into a saucer will ensure that only the tip of the brush is dipped into the paint, thereby eliminating the possibility of any 'runs'.

4 Using a fairly fine paintbrush, paint the squares and the main motifs. The larger motifs should be painted first and alternated, so that the colour is not smudged. Continue until all the shapes are painted and you are happy with the design.

5 Leave the shades to dry. To fix the paints 'blowdry' the shades with a hot hairdryer held quite close to them. Move the hairdryer evenly over the shades for several minutes, taking care not to burn the fabric.

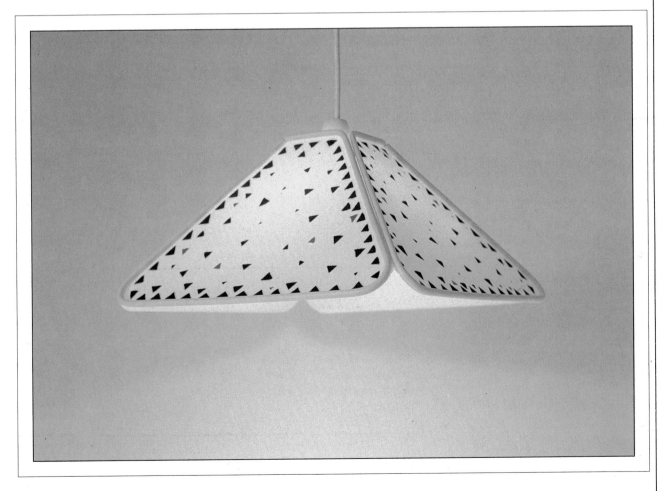

LACY CURTAINS AND BEDLINEN

Lace curtains at a bedroom window always give a soft, romantic look to the room. These curtains have been subtly dabbed with a very gentle shade of pink to co-ordinate with the bedlinen. Generally speaking, pastel colours are more compatible with lace than hard, primary colours. The delicate borders on the duvet (continental quilt) cover and pillowcases have been created by using a piece of lace cut from the length of curtain as a stencil to echo the pattern of the lace.

EQUIPMENT FOR CURTAINS

cotton lace
masking tape
fabric paints
water
clean saucers
sponge
clean cloth for ironing
iron to fix the paint

METHOD FOR CURTAINS

1 Stretch out as much of the lace as you can over a clean work surface and secure it down with masking tape.

2 Mix the fabric paint, diluting it with water until it has a watery consistency and is a pastel colour. It should be pale and soft so that it looks like a tint.

3 Dip the tip of the sponge into the diluted fabric paint, ensuring that the sponge is not too wet. Gently dab the sponge onto the lace curtain at intervals so that the colour is evenly spaced rather than giving all-over coverage.

4 Repeat the above process until the pattern is complete, working from one end of the fabric to the other. Leave the material to dry thoroughly on a flat surface.

5 Fix by ironing onto the painted side of the fabric with a medium hot iron, placing a clean cloth between the fabric and the iron.

TIPS

○ *Car spray paints can be used instead of fabric paints, as long as only a light film of paint lands on the fabric. Excessive use of the spray will make the material too stiff to use.*

○ *Only one side of the duvet cover needs to be painted. This will give you a choice of plain or patterned duvet, and save both on time and fabric paint.*

RIGHT: The lacy curtain, subtly dabbed with pink fabric paint, co-ordinates with the stencilled bedlinen. A piece of the lace curtain has been used as a stencil.

lace stencils

EQUIPMENT FOR BEDLINEN

cotton duvet (continental quilt) and
pillowcases
paper or plastic sheet to protect
pillowcases and duvet (continental
quilt) cover
fabric paint
piece of lace
masking tape
brush or sponge
clean cloth for ironing
iron to fix the paint

METHOD FOR BEDLINEN

1 Place a sheet of paper or
plastic inside the pillowcases
and the duvet (continental quilt)
cover to prevent the paint from
seeping through to the other side of
the bedlinen.

2 Using undiluted fabric paint, mix
the same shade as that used on
the tinted lace. A little red added to
lots of white will create a soft pink.

3 Cut the lace to the desired shape
and width of the border on the
pillowcases. This is a matter of taste,
but make sure that it is wide enough
for the pattern to be clearly seen.

4 Fasten the stencil onto the
pillowcase using masking tape.
Ensure that the positioning of the
masking tape will not interfere with
the pattern.

5 Dip the tip of the brush or
sponge into the paint. Dab the
paint onto the pillowcase through
the lace. The lace will act as a stencil,
leaving an imprint of its pattern. If the
sponge or brush is overloaded with
paint, the resulting pattern will not
be sharp enough.

6 Carefully remove the lace
stencil. Leave it to dry before
re-using it on the other pillowcase.

7 Repeat the above process on the
duvet (continental quilt) cover.
To save time, the lace motifs can be
well spaced out while still being very
effective. If you are short of working
space, paint the cover in sections,
allowing each section to dry before
moving on to the next.

8 When the paint is dry, fix it onto
the material by ironing onto the
painted side of the fabric with a hot
iron, placing a clean cloth between
the fabric and the iron.

BELOW: *Sponging fabric paint through a lace
stencil can create a wide variety of unusual
and pretty effects.*

GEOMETRIC SILK

The screen printing process is really a refinement of stencilling. With practice, lovely, even areas of colour can be obtained. The apparatus can be very inexpensive and is easy to make at home. It consists of a rectangular or square wooden frame, across which a fine gauze is stretched very tightly. Traditionally, the gauze used to be made out of silk and the process used to be called 'silk screen printing' but synthetic materials are now used. Ink is then forced through the mesh onto the fabric by using a squeegee. The areas of fabric where you do not want the colour to fall must be blocked off. Probably the simplest way of doing this is to apply varnish to the mesh and allow it to dry. The screen can then be used again and again to create identical prints. Different colourways can be used, as long as the screen is thoroughly washed before changing the inks. Allow the screen to dry completely before using it.

The beginner to this printing process should experiment with simple shapes and patterns such as circles and stripes in order to learn about this versatile technique. For example, simple strips of masking tape can be put directly onto the screen to create a stripe. Once this has been printed, the screen can be moved over the material to build up stripes of different thicknesses, or rotated to form a checked pattern.

For more pictorial designs, a paper stencil should be used. The pattern is cut out of the paper so that the areas to be printed are cut away, leaving the paper to act as a block, or resist, to the colour. Quite a fine detail can be achieved by using this method, but it is advisable to avoid intricate details, as the cut image will become very fragile.

Before you start, whether you are using masking tape, varnish or paper stencils, try the print out on sheets of paper or cotton fabric to make sure that all the areas surrounding the design are fully blocked using thick tape.

If you are creating an image which incorporates several colours, a separate screen will be required for each one. The beginner should not be over-ambitious in the use of colour.

The fabric design shown here is an ideal project to start on. The image is simple, but very effective, showing a flat, even colour distribution.

A homemade screen can be fashioned out of knot-free wood which is planed to a perfectly smooth finish. The smaller the screen you make, the more manageable it will be. It is very important that the finished frame should be flat so that an even print is obtained. The outside edges and corners of the frame should be rounded with sandpaper, and the inner edges left angled. A ready-made inexpensive screen can be bought from most art shops.

The fabric mesh is fastened to the screen with tacks. Drawing pins (thumb tacks) or strong staples can also be used. The mesh must be stretched as tightly as possible. The best way of doing this is to fasten the material to two points opposite each other in the centre of the two sides, then move outwards towards the corners. Carefully mask the edges of the screen, making a furrow at one end for the paint. A squeegee can be bought from an art shop, but a home-made version can be just as effective. Use a rubber draught excluder (stripping) and glue it between the pieces of hardboard (masonite).

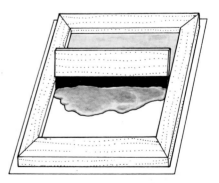

ABOVE: A small screen and squeegee can be bought or made for screen printing material. The printing ink is applied to the top of the screen and is forced across the screen, using the squeegee.

silk screen printing

EQUIPMENT

length of silk
protective blanket and sheeting for
    the work surface
masking tape
fabric paint
large piece of paper for use as a stencil
screen
squeegee
iron to fix the paints

METHOD

1 Prepare your work area, making sure that you have plenty of room and that the work surface is protected. The work surface should be well padded. This is best done by covering the table with a blanket, avoiding any seams which will affect the printing. The blanket should then be covered with a sheet or length of sheeting. Make sure that all your equipment is nearby.

2 Lay the fabric out flat, carefully removing any creases. It is essential that the fabric is perfectly smooth before you start printing on it, because any unevenness will cause the printing to be unsatisfactory. For a professional result, iron the fabric onto the padded work surface. Secure it to the work surface with masking tape. Mix the dyes, ensuring that you have blended enough. Test the colours on a piece of sample fabric before you start.

3 Cut a simple square out of a piece of paper. This will be used as a stencil to create your pattern. Make sure that the cut stencil fits within the screen and that there is sufficient space, top and bottom, for the ink well. It is essential that plenty of space is left around the cut area of the stencil or ink will seep through onto the fabric. Tape all the surrounding areas of the screen, leaving only the open square shape untaped for the colour printing.

4 Place a generous amount of printing colour in the well of the screen. The lightest colour—pink—should be printed first. Place the squeegee over the colour and draw it across the screen. Move the squeegee back to the well. Lift the screen off the fabric to reveal the printed square. Two pulls across the fabric are usually sufficient for cottons and silks, but a heavier fabric such as linen or hessian (burlap) will need three or four pulls.

5 Allow the pink squares to dry, then repeat the above process with the blue and then the grey.

6 Allow the fabric to dry completely. A hairdryer can be placed near the fabric to speed up the process, but make sure it is not held too close.

7 The paint can be made permanent in one of two ways. It can be fixed in the usual way by ironing onto the back of the fabric with a fairly hot iron, which can be very time-consuming if it is a large piece of fabric. Alternatively, the material can be neatly folded into a package and wrapped in a piece of cotton or foil. It can then placed into a pre-heated oven set on 180°C (350°F) for seven minutes. Allow it to cool before unwrapping.

TIPS

o *If you are not certain whether the screen has given a satisfactory paint coverage, hold one corner of the screen in place with the left hand and lift the opposite end of the screen with the right hand. This will enable you to look under the screen without disturbing the fabric. If the colour is uneven the screen can be lowered back down and a couple of extra pulls with the squeegee will make the colour denser. If the screen is completely removed from the fabric it is extremely difficult to replace it in exactly the same position.*

o *The printing might cause a light stiffening to the cloth. If so, it should be washed in lukewarm soap suds after the colour has been made permanent.*

LEFT: *This dramatic pattern has been created by using a very basic and easy screen printing technique. It is, therefore, an ideal project for the beginner to tackle.*

ROSES SCREEN

A very traditional rose design has been painted onto silk to fit within the antique fire screen. The roses are a perfect subject to enhance the elegant decor of the bedroom. Worked on a cream silk that has a slightly nubbly texture, the roses are painted in subtle colours that are reminiscent of old faded fabrics from a bygone age.

Take great care when mixing the paints to achieve the right colour balance. Dilute the colours with water or add white to change the tones to more pastel shades. Silk paints should be used for this project. They can be mixed with each other and water can be added, but they are not compatible with any other types of paint.

Use a fairly heavyweight silk for the screen. A light, fine silk will be much more difficult to paint on and the paints will spread out and bleed into the fabric. Although bleeding can create lovely results, this is not the desired effect for this project.

A degree of skill is necessary to paint the roses as realistically as the ones in the picture, but with care and the correct colour combination, the same effect can be achieved. Tracing roses and cutting a stencil may be easier. However, if stencilling, silk paints cannot be used as they are too watery and will seep under the edges of the stencil. Fabric paints will have to be used instead, but they will not give the same quality of finish.

When painting by hand, a selection of brushes must be used for different stroke effects. Use scraps of fabrics to try out different effects.

RIGHT: Soft, traditional roses painted on silk are always a perfect complement to antique furniture.

EQUIPMENT

heavyweight silk
masking tape
silk paints
clean saucers
pencil or tailor's chalk
selection of fine artist's brushes
clean cloth for ironing
iron to fix the paints (check the
    manufacturer's instructions)

METHOD

1 Stretch out the fabric on a flat working surface and secure it down with masking tape.

2 Mix the colours, making sure that they have all been tested on the appropriate fabric and that they co-ordinate. Mix enough of each colour to complete the design.

3 Draw the design on the silk, using a pencil or tailor's chalk. Centre the design, leaving enough fabric around the edge so that the piece fits into the screen without any of the design disappearing into the edge of the screen.

4 Start by painting all the leaves that are the same colour. This will cut down on washing out the brush too often. Load the brush with dark grey paint and spread it out as much as possible. Paint so that the edges are darker than the centres of the leaves. Where the leaves are in two sections, leave a gap so that a white line is evident between the two leaf sections. This is to break up the solid areas and allow background colour to show through.

5 Wash and dry the brush carefully. Use light grey for the other leaves and then darker grey for the fine veins on the leaves. Wash and dry the brush between each change of colour, to prevent the paints from becoming muddy.

6 Paint the roses, varying the shades of colour within each rose. The edges of the roses should be darker, with white (background colour) between the petals.

7 Fix the paint. This is usually done by ironing, but read the paint manufacturer's instructions carefully beforehand as some silk paints need to be steam-fixed.

TIPS

o *Drawing the roses on the silk can be simplified by sketching the design to scale on a piece of paper. Place the drawing underneath the fabric and trace it onto the fabric. If the silk is not transparent, hold it up to the window. The light shining through the fabric will ensure that the outline is clearly visible.*

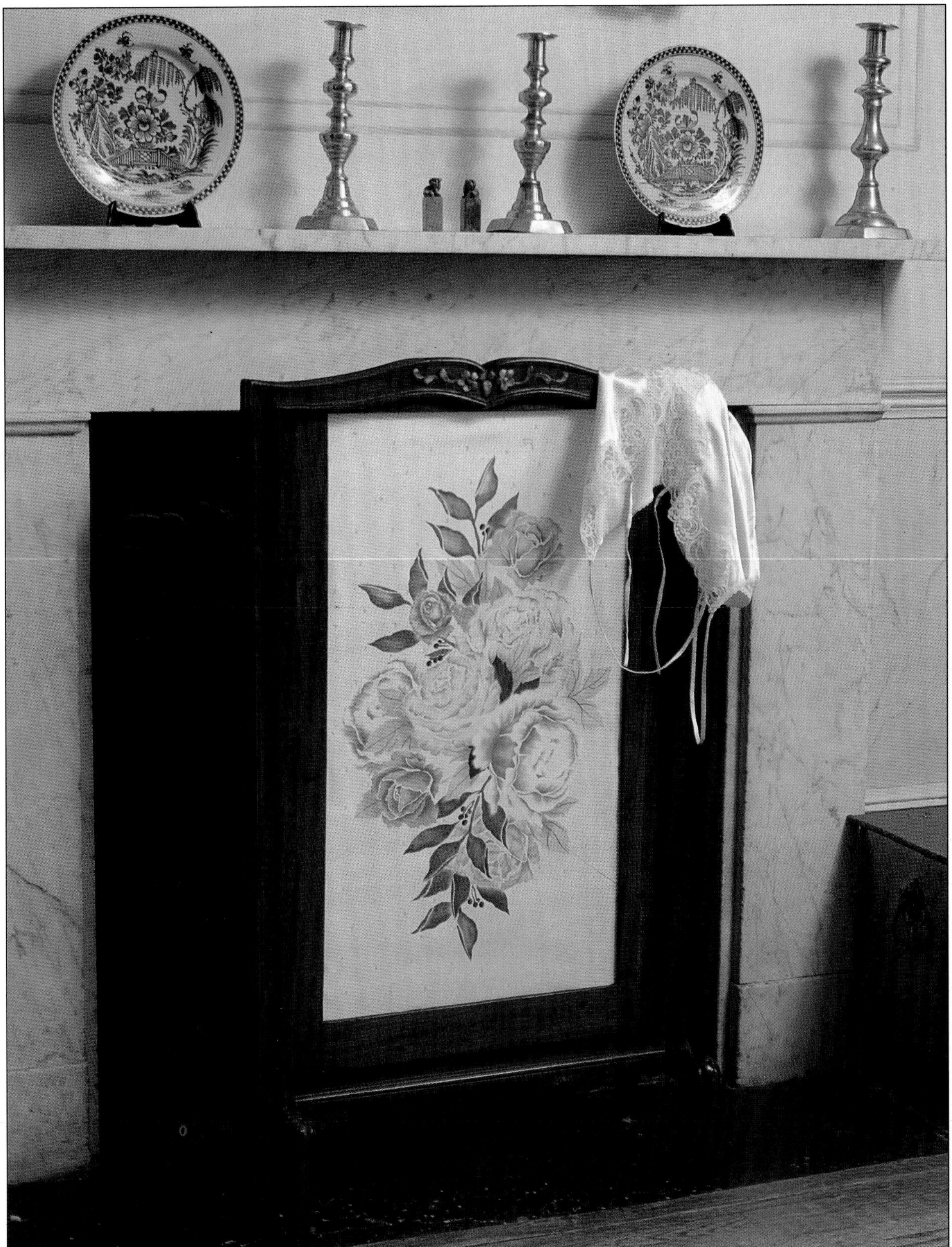

PINK LAMPSHADE

Plain fabric lampshades in soft pale colours are plentiful in the shops and are inexpensive to buy. They can be personalized and decorated in a multitude of imaginative ways to add interest to the bedside table. Freehand designs can be carefully drawn onto a shade, using fine artist's brushes or, for stronger effect, use thick bold strokes in primary colours. They can also be sprayed in a variety of ways, using a toothbrush, or spattered with the colours of your choice.

The delicate, almost marbled texture of this lampshade was achieved by a sponging process. Natural sponges give the best results for this technique. As an alternative, an ordinary, man-made sponge can be used, or a crumpled up clean rag.

LEFT: A plain lampshade can be quickly and inexpensively decorated using a household brush or natural sponge, lightly dipped in pastel coloured fabric paints.

RIGHT: Experiment with a variety of colour combinations on sketches before sponging the shade. This gentle, delicate technique can make unlikely colour combinations complement each other beautifully.

EQUIPMENT

fabric lampshade
fabric paints
glitter paints (optional)
clean saucers
natural sponge or crumpled rag
hairdryer

METHOD

1 Pour the fabric paints into clean saucers and lightly dip the sponge or rag into the paint. It is important that not too much paint is applied to the sponge or rag, as a thick blob of colour without any texture will result.

2 Starting with the main colour of your design, lightly dab the lampshade all over, leaving an even gap between each dab. Use different areas of the sponge when pressing down onto the shade to vary the tones and textures of the pattern. Rinse the sponge and leave it to dry.

3 Apply the second layer of colour to the shade, repeating the above process. Allow the colours to merge to create overlaps and new tones. Continue to apply layers of colour until you are satisfied with the coverage and the colour distribution.

4 Leave the lampshade to dry. Fix the paints by 'blow drying' the shade for several minutes with a hot hairdryer. Hold the dryer fairly close to the shade, without burning it.

TIPS

o *Always wash the sponge and allow it to dry before changing colour. A wet sponge may leave dull, dirty-looking marks on the shade.*

o *When sponging, start with the palest colours first, graduating to the darker shades, as these will be difficult disguise if they are applied too freely.*

o *Glitter paints can be very effectively used on sponged fabrics. They should be dabbed on as a final coat.*

FLORAL PRINT

The idea for this floral piece was taken from seed catalogues and old gardening magazines. A selection of favourite images were cut from gardening sources and then made into a large collage. The image was then photocopied and used for the transfer printing process.

The choice of subject for transfer printing is entirely personal. Hobbies or interests such as trains, cars, fishing or sailing can all be transferred onto fabric. This quick and easy technique involves transferring an image which has been drawn on newsprint onto fabric. Man-made materials such as polyester are ideal for this method and will ensure a beautiful, translucent quality to the colour. Lighter, paler effects are achieved on natural fabrics.

This process allows for multiple colours to be used in one application without the colours becoming dull or muddy. For instance, yellow over blue will give emerald or lime green, yellow over pink will produce a warm orange, pink over blue will create purple.

EQUIPMENT

length of man-made fabric such as
    polyester
protective paper and fabric
transfer paints
containers for mixing the paints
newsprint
selection of artist's brushes
water and clean rags
iron to transfer the paints

TIPS

o *Newsprint paper can be used for several applications. Each time it is used, the colour becomes a tone lighter. Up to six applications can be made before the colour effect is exhausted.*

o *Threads or yarns placed between the paper and the fabric will create a linear effect. Pieces of netting will give a gauze-like quality to the work.*

LEFT The bright images of this hanging were created by using transfer paints. These paints can be blended without the colours becoming dull or muddy.

METHOD

1 Prepare the work area. No elaborate preparations are necessary for this technique—simply cover a flat surface with protective paper or sheeting.

2 Mix the dyes. Transfer paints are available in an interesting selection of colours. By adding water to them the tones can be adjusted. For example, red mixed with water will make pink, black mixed with water will make grey. The colours can also be blended with each other to produce new shades.

3 Prepare the design image to scale on the newsprint. In this case, the image was made up from photocopies of flowers. Using artist's brushes, paint your image onto the newsprint dipping the brush lightly into the paint. Once you are happy with the result, allow it to dry.

4 Heat the iron to a high temperature. Trial pieces of fabric should be tested to obtain the correct temperature. If the iron is too hot the fabric will burn, if it is not hot enough the colours will lack their full strength.

5 Cover the ironing board with inexpensive fabric. Lay the polyester on top of it and then place the paper design face down onto the fabric. Apply the iron to the fabric. The amount of time needed will have been ascertained on your test strip, but by peeling back the corner of the paper, the penetration of colour can be assessed. Simply increasing the time will give a deeper colour effect. The colour, when dry on the paper bears no similarity to the actual results on the fabric, which are rich and bright.

6 When the design has been ironed all over, carefully peel off the newsprint.

7 The image on this wall hanging was achieved by reapplying of the paper image over and over again. A second image was then drawn and applied to the textural, mixed colour image already on the fabric.

8 The design colour is fixed in the process of application, and no extra fixing is required.

tie and dye

ZEBRA-EFFECT BEDSPREAD

This very traditional method of dyeing is quick, cheap and can produce startlingly beautiful results. Tones of colour fade and merge into patterns and textures, resulting in a unique piece of fabric. No matter how conscientiously you try to repeat a pattern, it will be impossible to make an identical piece of fabric.

Tie dyeing can be mastered by anyone because it requires no artistic skills whatsoever. All that you have to do is tie pieces of string around the fabric and immerse it in dye. Even if the result is not what you expected, the 'mistake' will often be a happy one, giving the fabric a quality which could not have been planned or foreseen.

Before you start, it is important to ensure that the article to be dyed has been thoroughly washed. This will remove any special finishes on the fabric or any buildup of dirt which would hinder dye penetration. It should also be remembered that you can only dye to a darker colour than the original. To ensure a good, clear colour, the fabric should be white, cream or a soft pastel shade to begin with. Patterned fabrics are not at all suitable for this method. A better result will also be achieved by using a lightweight, closely woven fabric. A textured or heavy fabric will not take the dye well and the resulting patterning will be indistinct.

There are many ways of tying the fabric up to produce different effects. Experimenting with pleats, ruching, knotting and binding is half the fun of this technique. However, it is important to bear in mind that a crisp, definite result will not occur unless the fabric is tied really tightly before immersing it in dye.

RIGHT: This beautiful bedspread has been created by using the traditional tie and dye technique. By choosing colours that are compatible with the decor of the room, and the technique itself—shades of blue or rich, earthy colours—the finished article can be a startlingly lovely and original focal point in the room.

EQUIPMENT

cotton bedspread or thick sheet
scales to weigh the fabric
string
large bucket or container for dyeing
rubber gloves
cold water dye and manufacturer's
    recommended fixing agents
wooden stick or spoon for stirring
scissors

METHOD

1 To make a striped effect, crease the fabric into accordion pleats from end to end. This will be easier if the fabric is slightly dampened first. However, don't make it too wet.

2 Tie the pleated fabric at intervals with string securing each one tightly. The untied areas will take the full effect of the dye and will be the darkest in colour. The fabric can be tied at regular intervals or randomly —this is a matter of personal preference.

3 Once you have tied up the fabric, make sure that it has been done neatly and that the knots are secure.

4 Wearing rubber gloves, mix the dye according to the manufacturer's instructions. Make sure that the container you use is large enough for the fabric you are dyeing. The fabric must have plenty of room to circulate so that the colour can penetrate freely.

5 Wet the fabric, then place the bedspread into the dye container. Stir frequently with a wooden spoon or stick for the first 30 minutes to ensure that the colour is evenly distributed. Only stir occasionally after that. Leave the fabric in the container for the recommended length of time. Do not be tempted to remove it too soon.

6 When the dyeing time is up, rinse the fabric in clean water until the water runs clear. This will take several rinses.

7 Remove the string with sharp scissors, taking great care not to cut the material itself. Unravel the fabric and hang it up, preferably outside, to dry.

TIPS

o *Launder the bedspread separately for the first three washes to ensure that any loose dye does not spoil the rest of your washing.*

The soft furnishings in this children's room have been effectively co-ordinated by spattering fabric paints on the crib cover and acrylic paints over the window blind.

PLAYING

Children's rooms provide endless scope for fabric painting. The main consideration when designing for the playroom is that the fabrics should be suited to their purpose. There is no point in decorating pretty, delicate silks and sheer fabrics when washability and durability are of prime importance in a child's room. Remember that it is likely to be a play area as well as a sleep area and spills of all kinds are inevitable. Hard wearing cottons are perhaps the best type of fabrics to use from the point of view of durability and they are also relatively inexpensive and easy to work on.

Bedcovers, curtains or blinds and cushion covers can all be painted to co-ordinate or contrast with existing elements such as the carpet or wallpaper. Stencilled motifs can be used as a border or as an all-over design, and large items such as curtains or bedcovers can be spattered or splashed for an instant abstract design, perhaps with your child's assistance. Other items, such as dressing gowns and teddies' or dolls' clothes, can be painted to match.

In addition to adding instant individuality to new items, painting can give a new lease of life to old, well-worn and washed out articles, as well as being an inexpensive way to add a lift to the room without going to the trouble of complete redecoration.

Bold colours and shapes are ideal for children's rooms and subtlety is definitely *not* the keyword. Design inspiration can be found from a wide variety of sources. Cartoon and comic book characters can be traced from books and then made into stencils. Animals of all kinds are always popular and can also be traced, simplified and made into stencils, as can numbers and letters of the alphabet. In fact the only limiting factor to design inspiration is your own imagination, and if this is the case, the children will be only too willing to oblige!

Children of all ages, however young, enjoy drawing and painting with colour. Uninhibited by pre-conceived ideas about their own abilities and 'Art', they will create original and beautiful effects, playing with shapes and colours. Decorating fabrics for their own room will be particularly pleasurable and rewarding as the item will be practical and in daily use. Decorating scatter cushions is an ideal way for a child to learn about fabric painting on. Sponging, spattering and painting can be tackled by very young children, although it is always a good idea to protect the surrounding work area and clothing. Older children can be taught simple printing techniques—lino printing and stencilling will soon be mastered and thoroughly enjoyed.

CO-ORDINATING BLIND AND CRIB COVER

Spatter painting has given an bright co-ordinated look to this children's room. The use of primary colours adds to the naive, simple effect and also means that the colour tones do not have to be matched. The vivid colours are very effective in the plain surroundings.

Spatter painting is ideal for those with little confidence in their technical ability, because it is so quick and easy to do. However, it is a very messy technique which should, ideally be done outside, or in a large area with the surrounding surfaces carefully covered up.

The colours for the roller blind and the crib cover are exactly the same, although the blind is painted with acrylic paints and fabric paints are used for the crib cover.

This choice of paints was made because blinds are difficult to iron and the fabric paints cannot, therefore, be made permanent. Although blinds are not usually washed, condensation could cause the fabric paint to bleed. Acrylic paints are waterproof so they will be permanent once painted onto the blind.

BELOW: In addition to using fabric paints in primary colours, this sampler has incorporated textured plastic-finish paints in the striking pattern. The long, straight quality of the splashes has been created by using a stick rather than brushes for flicking the paint.

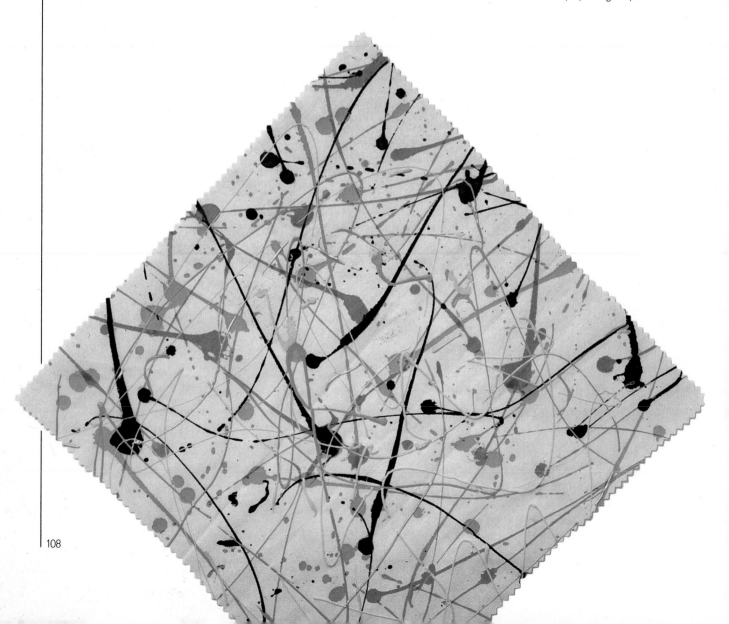

EQUIPMENT FOR THE ROLLER BLIND

fabric roller blind
protective newspaper or sheeting for
    the work area
acrylic paints
stick or the end of a brush for flicking
    the paint
rags for wiping the stick

METHOD FOR THE ROLLER BLIND

1 Cover all surrounding areas with sheeting or newspaper.

2 The blind should be painted flat, not at a window, because the paint will drip if it is in a vertical position.

3 As you are using primary colours, you can work straight from the pots. Dip the end of the stick into the pot, ensuring that it is not overloaded with paint. Flick the paint onto the blind, using a quick, downwards motion from the wrist. Start with the palest colours first, wiping the end of the stick before changing colours. Continue flicking on the paint until the blind is quite densely covered.

4 Allow the blind to dry flat. It may appear to be a bit creased when it is returned to the window, but these creases will soon drop out.

TIPS

o *If you are making your own blind out of canvas or cotton, fabric paints can be used as they can easily be ironed.*

o *Children can help with this project as it is the easiest of all the fabric painting techniques. Keep a close watch over them to ensure that no accidents occur.*

EQUIPMENT FOR THE CRIB COVER

cotton crib cover
protective sheeting or newspaper for
    the work area
fabric paints
stick or the end of a brush for
    flicking the paint
rags for wiping the stick
clean cloth for ironing
iron to fix the paints

METHOD FOR CRIB COVER

1 Cover all surrounding areas with sheeting or newspaper. Although fabric paint is easily wiped off from most surfaces, it may be difficult to remove from upholstery or carpets.

2 Place the crib cover onto your working area. There is no need to fix it down as it is quite heavy and will not slip.

3 Spatter the crib cover as directed for the blind. This technique is often referred to as 'action' painting, so let the finished result reflect the title. Flicking the paint from different directions will result in a more exciting design.

4 Blot any excess paint on the cover with newspaper or a piece of clean fabric. This will speed up the drying time and prevent the paint from becoming too thick on the cover.

5 When dry, fix the paint by placing a clean cloth over the painted cover. Iron over it with a hot iron. The paint will now be permanent.

BELOW: These samplers vividly portray the exciting results that can be achieved by using this very simple technique. Bright, bold colours are nearly always more effective for spatter painting than more subtle shades.

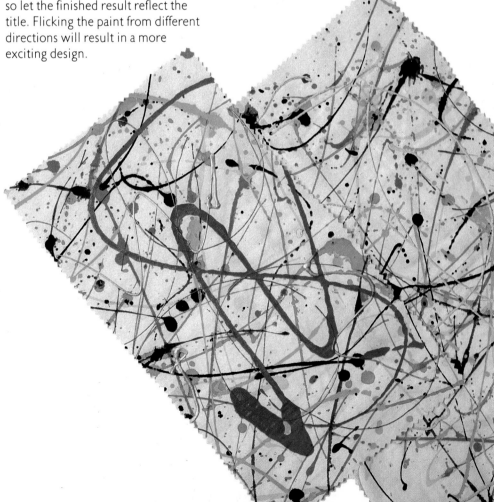

CHILDREN'S CUSHIONS

The child-like quality of these cushions was created by using fabric crayons and puff paints. The crayons are available in a good range of strong, bright colours, rather like children's wax crayons, and the puff paints add a textural interest as the paint swells up when it is ironed.

   The simple, naive designs were based upon children's art. Although they were worked out beforehand using felt tip pens, there is no need to be too precise—an intuitive approach to colour and pattern can yield very satisfying results.

EQUIPMENT

white cotton, cut to the required
   cushion size
felt tip pens and paper to sketch the
   designs beforehand (optional)
masking tape
fabric crayons
puff paints
clean cloths for ironing
iron to fix the paints

METHOD

1 If you do not feel confident enough to work straight onto the material, sketch your ideas beforehand.

2 Using a pencil draw the design, one cushion at a time, onto the fabric using the fabric crayons. Follow the pencil outline of the design.

3 The fabric crayons will be easier to use if the fabric is taut. Stretch it out on the work surface and secure with masking tape.

4 Add the textural detail using the puff paints. The paints are applied through a nozzle, so it is easy to create linear effects. They can be applied on top of the crayons or at random over the material.

5 Once the paints have dried, lay the painted fabric over a covered ironing surface, face down. Iron the back of the design using slow, even pressure. Repeat for each cushion, replacing the ironing cloth when necessary. Make the cushions.

TIPS

o *Let your own children create the designs for the cushions. The results will be original and charming. Keep a close eye on them though, to make sure that the paint is only being applied to the cushions!*

o *Do not apply puff paints too thickly or they will peel off the material.*

o *Fabric crayons can easily smudge, so fix them by ironing before using the puff paints.*

These bright and colourful cushions will add character and appeal to the children's room. They have been drawn using a combination of fabric crayons and puff pens, giving them an unusual textured quality. The preliminary sketches were made in felt pens, working out the design shapes and colour combinations. Strong primary colours should be used to enhance the child-like quality of the work.

potato prints

ETHNIC TOY CHEST AND TOY BAG

The designs for this toy chest and toy bag were largely inspired by the traditions of ethnic art from many diverse cultures and countries such as the Yoruba tribes of West Africa, the Mayan Indians of Mexico and the white-washed and sun bleached architecture found in remote Grecian villages and other undiscovered corners of the Mediterranean.

These motifs have a directness and a simplicity that is a reflection of ancient society's needs to represent a physical world where animals and plants were often imbued with a magical significance that was an important part of their cultures.

The lining of the toy chest and the toy bag were both made out of calico (muslin). The toy bag is simply made by stitching two rectangular pieces of fabric together. The drawstring has been fashioned from coarse hemp to emphasize the ethnic quality of the project. To make the toy box lining, stretch the fabric over thin board which has been accurately cut to the correct dimensions of the interior of the box. The boards are then pinned to the inside of the toy box. In both cases, the fabric must be painted beforehand.

TIPS

o *If you lack the confidence to tackle painting the designs freehand, trace the image that you want to use—from a book, magazine etc. —onto tracing paper, using charcoal. Turn the tracing paper over onto the fabric, so that it is charcoal-side down, and gently rub the back of the tracing paper, using a spoon. This will leave a soft outline on the fabric to be filled in. Alternatively, stencils can be used, but experiment on scraps of your fabric first, before actually starting the project.*

LEFT. The simple, child-like decoration on this toy bag has been created by using a combination of potato prints and hand-painted images.

EQUIPMENT

paper and pencil
calico (muslin)
potato
masking tape
fabric paints
clean saucers
selection of fine artist's brushes
clean cloth for ironing
iron to fix the paints

BELOW: The playroom is an ideal place to experiment with themes and images which might be too overpowering in the living room. Here, strong ethnic images, executed in subtle colours have been used to decorate the calico toy bag and toy chest.

METHOD

1 Experiment with ethnic images from art books and travel literature, until you find a motif you want to work around. Once you are happy with your design, draw it to scale on a piece of paper making sure that the proportions are correct. You may want to indicate on the fabric where the motifs will fall, using a soft pencil.

2 The repeated motif was inspired by an Ashanti shield decoration. This was achieved by using a potato cut in half. Leave the cut potato to dry for half an hour to get rid of any excess moisture.

3 Stretch the fabric out on your working surface and fix it down firmly with masking tape.

4 Use a brush to cover the flat side of the potato with a thin film of paint. Do not use too much paint, or you will create uneven borders around each print. It is best to pour the paint into a saucer to avoid overloading the brush.

5 Press the potato firmly onto the fabric. Only reapply the paint on alternate prints to avoid a blotchy effect. Repeat until the design is complete.

6 The animals are painted freehand, using fine artist's brushes. Leave the fabric to dry away from direct heat.

7 Fix the dye in place by ironing onto the painted side of the fabric with a hot iron, placing a cloth between the fabric and the iron.

freestyle painting

CHILDREN'S LAMPSHADE

A quick but effective way to add something special to a child's room is to customize a fabric lampshade by painting it with a simple, geometric design. A lampshade is an easy surface to paint and is certainly not time-consuming. It is also a cheap and effective way of transforming an ordinary shade into a unique piece of decoration which has been specially designed for a particular room. A strong, simple image can be the focal point in a room and added interest is created when the light shines through it, emphasizing the pattern.

This design is based on a simple leaf shape, which has been stylized and painted in bright colours with a black outline.

EQUIPMENT

fabric lampshade
pencil
paper
tape measure
fabric paints
clean saucers
selection of artist's brushes
hairdryer

METHOD

1 Sketch the leaf shapes on paper until you have finalized your design. The two shapes used on the lampshade are the same, but one is larger than the other.

2 Using the tape measure, work out where the motifs are going to appear on the lampshade. They should be evenly spaced so that the small leaf fits between the larger ones. Indicate lightly in pencil where each motif will appear.

3 Cut the leaf shapes out of the paper. Trace around the shapes onto the shade. This will be much quicker and easier than copying the designs onto the shade.

4 Mix the fabric paints in the saucers. Make sure that the colour tones are compatible before you start.

5 Using a fine brush, paint all the black outlines. The lines are not straight and will look more interesting if they are spontaneous brush strokes that are a little uneven. Paint the motifs alternately, so that they do not smudge as you work. Allow the paint to dry.

6 Leaving a narrow outline of background colour, fill in the solid shapes, using a thicker brush to achieve a flat surface. Allow the paint to dry.

7 Fix the paints by 'blowdrying' the shades with a hot hairdryer held quite close to them.

TIPS

o *If the colour is patchy, allow it to dry and apply a second coat to give the paint more depth.*

RIGHT: *Even a relatively small area of fabric, such as a lampshade, can be transformed into a stylish accessory using contemporary images painted in strong colours.*

plastic paints

GRAFFITI CUSHIONS

These cushions are quick and fun to decorate. The 'graffiti' can be made up of pop star's names, children's rhymes, pet's names etc, combined in random patterns. These designs have been painted directly onto ready-made cushions using paints straight from the tube. However, it is necessary to practise this technique on scraps of fabric until you are confident of maintaining the correct pressure on the tube to produce an even line of paint. The background colour of the cushion can be as bright or as dark as you choose, as the paint will not sink into the fabric, but will remain on the surface of the cushion covers.

EQUIPMENT

coloured cushion covers
newspaper or fabric to protect your
    work surface
clean sheets of paper—not
    newspaper
soft pencil or tailor's chalk
masking tape
plastic paints

METHOD

1 If the cushions are new, wash out any manufacturer's finish or the paint will not adhere to the surface of the fabric. If the cushion covers are old, make sure that they are clean, dry and greasefree.

2 Prepare a clean area to work on. Cover it with old fabric or paper, as plastic paints are very difficult to remove from most surfaces.

3 Place a clean sheet of paper between the back and the front of the inside of the cushion so that the back of the fabric is not marked when the front is painted.

4 Work out your design on a piece of paper cut to the same size as the cushion covers. The letters, numbers and words should be drawn freehand, but the design will be more pleasing if the characters are fairly evenly spaced.

5 Once you are happy with your design, transfer it onto the fabric using tailor's chalk or a soft pencil. These will wash out.

6 Stretch the fabric onto the work surface using masking tape to fix it down at each corner.

7 Press the nozzle of the paint tube against the fabric and gently squeeze it until a fine line of paint appears. Paint each motif carefully with flowing lines. If the paint appears to become thick, wipe the nozzle of the tube and continue. Avoid any seams in the material as they may encourage blobs of paint.

8 Once you are happy with your design, leave the cushion covers to dry. The paint is now permanent and will need no extra fixing.

TIPS

o *Wash the cushion covers carefully in lukewarm water for the first few washes.*

o *Paint alternate characters on the cushions, to avoid smudging adjacent, newly-painted letters or numbers.*

Cushions are always fun in the playroom. Plastic paints give you—and the children— the opportunity to decorate them with all kinds of images. Names, numbers and simple shapes can all be utilized in the designs. This is also an ideal way of introducing children to the fun and excitement of making things for the home.

*Simple, but colourful designs can liven up the plainest of bathrooms
by adding a touch of fun as well as colour
to bathroom accessories.*

WASHING

The bathroom is probably the one solely functional room in the house and, as such, is often neglected when it comes down to decoration. However, there is much scope for adding character in the form of painted fabrics, for instance, towels, bathmats, curtains etc.

When deciding on your design, it is important to take into consideration the size of your bathroom. It is all too easy to overpower the existing decor with too enthusiastic an approach to painted fabric accessories. However, a little careful planning can transform a plain, characterless room.

Perhaps the most obvious and easy item to decorate is the window covering. It can be spattered or sponged or more formally painted. Inspiration can be taken from such sources as the seashore—shells, pebbles, seaweed all adapt beautifully to a bathroom setting. Keeping to the theme of the sea, muted watery colours can be used, although this need not necessarily mean 'washed out' colours. Envisage the sea in all its forms—calm, stormy, the vivid blue of the Mediterranean or the angry grey of the Atlantic. Take a look at some traditional Japanese prints—a watery theme is often in evidence.

Another theme that can be exploited is the decoration on ancient Greek and Roman pottery, with their highly stylized and simplistic motifs and glorious colours such as terracotta, turquoise, black and cream. The motifs can be translated straight into sophisticated border patterns. An all-over sponged effect as a base adds a touch of authenticity to these ancient designs.

This detailed approach cannot be translated so easily into heavily textured materials such as bathmats or towels, where a bright, less subtle approach will be easier to execute.

Making mistakes when working on fabric and towelling can be costly and very disappointing. Mistakes usually occur because insufficient time has been spent on developing your initial ideas. Experimenting with images on paper before embarking upon any fabric work will give you confidence as well as maturing your ideas for the project. Paints and shapes should then be tested on appropriate pieces of fabric.

Although simple examples of fabric painting and dyeing are given in this section, the potential for developing more complex designs will grow with your confidence in your ability to execute them.

BATHROOM SLIPPERS

The bathroom slippers illustrated on the previous page were transformed by painting them with a simple, multi-coloured chessboard effect.

EQUIPMENT

cotton slippers
large sheet of paper
pencil
children's crayons or felt tip pens
fabric felt tip pens
glitter paints
hairdryer to fix the paints

METHOD

1 Lay the slippers on a piece of paper which is larger than the slippers. Draw around the slippers using a pencil to give you an exact indication of their shape and size. Fill in the drawn shapes using ordinary felt tips or crayons. Try different colour combinations until you are satisfied with your design.

2 Using your sketch as a guideline, paint a grid over the slippers, including the underneath and the inside using a black fabric felt tip pen.

3 Fill in the grid using fabric felt tip pens to copy your design onto the slippers. Glitter paints can also be used for variety.

4 Fix the paints by using a hot hairdryer. 'Blow dry' them for several minutes to ensure that the paint is firmly fixed.

BATHMAT

This is a fun idea for the bathroom. Although the surface of the mat is textured, simple geometrics look very effective on this small area. As a bathmat will spend quite a lot of its life wet or damp, it is not a good idea to cover it in thick fabric paint. Instead, dots and small geometric stripes were created, using felt-tip fabric pens for a lighter, less dense result.

EQUIPMENT

cotton bathmat
large piece of paper
pencil
fabric felt tip pens
ruler
clean cloth for ironing
iron to fix the paint

TIPS

o *Always use a more watery type of paint, such as fabric felt tip pens, when working on a textured surface. A thick paint will make the fabric matted.*

BELOW AND LEFT: These sketches are part of a series which were worked out before the bathmat and slippers were painted. The idea was to make them as interesting and colourful as possible.

METHOD

1 Draw the pattern to scale on a piece of paper. A bathmat is not a large area, so this will not take long.

2 Using the drawing as a guideline, transfer the pattern onto the bathmat, using the fabric felt tip pens. A ruler can be used, but perfectly straight lines are impossible to achieve on such a textured surface. Paint the border first, then roughly fill in the squares using black, to create a chessboard effect.

3 Using the selection of coloured fabric felt tips, draw dashes over the central area. They may have to be painted over a few times to ensure that the colour is dark enough to show up. Try to keep the dashes evenly spread out.

4 Once you are happy with your design, leave the mat to dry. Cover the mat with a clean cloth and fix the paint by ironing evenly over the surface for a several minutes with a hot iron.

dyeing

BATHROOM TOWELS

Fabric dyes are a quick, easy and inexpensive way of giving a new lease of life to household fabrics whose original brightness has faded with age or to revamp whites which have become discoloured — towels, sheets and tablecloths are obvious candidates. It is also a good solution for items which have been washed with non-fast coloured fabrics and become patchy or discoloured.

There are two types of dye available for hand dyeing — cold water dyes and hot water dyes. Hot water dyes are really only suitable if you are using a washing machine. However, not all machines are suitable for dyeing because too much water passes through them, giving a pale end result.

Cold water dyes can only be used for natural fabrics, and are ideal for items such as towels and sheets, although the density of the colour will, of course, depend upon the fabric you are working on. Any polyester content in the fabric will result in a paler colour when dyed.

It is essential that the manufacturer's instructions are read and carefully followed when dyeing and that you buy enough dye for the weight of the item that you are going to colour.

These towels are a perfect example of how a fabric can be given an exciting new look by dyeing. White towels tend to lose their brilliance with age, while being in otherwise good condition. Dyeing them with a bright new colour to blend with the bathroom decor will make them look brand new and is inexpensive and easy to do. Pastel towels can also be overdyed to make the colours more vibrant, or they can be dramatically transformed into black or charcoal.

If the towels are a fairly strong colour, this will play a major part in the end result. For example, if the towel is yellow, a blue dye will result in green, and a red towel dyed blue will result in purple. If the towel is multi-coloured, all the colours will change, either slightly or dramatically, and this must be taken into account before dyeing. These colour changes should be tested beforehand by mixing fabric paints or poster paints. Some colours will not give a successful end result.

RIGHT: Towels can be successfully dyed to enhance the colour scheme in a newly-decorated bathroom. A deep blue was selected for these towels to accentuate the soft colour of the bathroom suite. Using a cold water dye on cotton will ensure a strong result.

dyeing

EQUIPMENT

cotton towels
scales
large bucket or container for dyeing
cold water dye and manufacturer's
recommended fixing agent
wooden stick or spoon for stirring
rubber gloves

METHOD

1 Check that the towels are 100% cotton. Any polyester content will result in a paler colour when dyed. If the towels have polyester edges, these areas will not dye at all.

2 Weigh the dry towels. This is important as the dry weight of the article determines how much dye will be used. Cold water dyes are particularly good for towels, as they result in an excellent strength of colour and will withstand frequent washing.

3 Wash and rinse the towels thoroughly, ensuring that they are clean and greasefree.

4 Mix the dye according to the manufacturer's instructions in the dye bucket or container. Add the damp towels.

5 Stir frequently with a wooden spoon or stick for the first thirty minutes to ensure that the dye is evenly distributed. Only stir occasionally after that.

6 Leave the towels in the dye for the recommended length of time. Remember that wet fabric looks several shades darker than dry fabric, so don't be tempted to remove the items before they are ready.

7 When the recommended time is over, rinse the towels thoroughly until the water runs clear, then wash them in very hot water using your usual washing powder. Rinse well.

8 Dry the towels away from direct sunlight or heat. Do not tumble dry or hang over a radiator.

TIPS

o *Make sure that the container you use for dyeing is large enough for the dye to penetrate freely. If it is too small, the end result will be patchy or streaky.*

o *It is advisable to wash the dyed towels separately the first time to make sure that they do not spoil the rest of your wash.*

ABOVE: Over-dyeing can sometimes give lovely effects. A blue and white towel has been over-dyed with yellow, producing a vivid green and yellow stripe.

BELOW: Old, tired-looking white towels have been given a new lease of life with a red dye.

PAINTED **T**OWEL AND **B**ATHROBE

A plain white towel and bathrobe can be painted to co-ordinate with each other. Once painted, these items would be equally at home on the beach or in the bathroom. The unusual motifs on the towel are based on snail shells, which have been stylized and strongly defined in vivid colours and black. Bold, bright accessories are always very successful in a white or pale grey bathroom.

BELOW: This boldly decorated towel will look just as good on the beach as in the bathroom. Its chequer-board border links its design to the bathrobe (overleaf).

hand-painting

EQUIPMENT

cotton bathrobe and towel
masking tape
yellow tailor's chalk
fabric paints
clean saucers for mixing
fabric felt tip pens
pencil
fine artist's brush
thick cardboard
clean cloth for ironing
iron to fix the paint

METHOD

1 Remove the belt of the bathrobe and place it to one side. Stretch out both the bathrobe and the towel on your working surface. If the items are to match, it is important to work on them together. Secure them firmly down with masking tape before painting.

2 Sketch the design onto the robe and towel using yellow tailor's chalk. This should be followed as a guideline.

3 Mix enough paint for both the bathrobe and the towel. Some of the black lines can be painted using a fabric felt tip pen.

4 Draw on the lines for the black chessboard edges using a fabric felt tip pen. Paint in the squares using felt tip pens or fabric paint. If the felt tip pens appear too faint in areas, the colour can be deepened by using a fine brush dipped into fabric paint. Do not overload the brush.

5 Use a black felt tip pen to paint the curved stems onto each pocket and at each end of the towel. Again, fabric paint can be used to deepen the colour. Using a clean artist's brush, paint three green dashes on each side of the curved line.

6 Paint a wavy line down the full length of the bathrobe belt and down each lapel, using a felt-tip pen. Paint red and green dots alternately along the wavy line.

7 Cut two circles from thick cardboard making one 2cm (¾ in) smaller than the other one.

8 Using a black fabric felt tip pen, draw the outline of the circles, placing one inside the other at regular intervals over the central area of the towel. Paint in each circle using red, green and yellow fabric paint, making sure that you do not smudge the black outlines.

9 Leave the bathrobe and towel to dry, then fix the paint by covering the items with a clean cloth and ironing evenly over the surface for a few minutes with a hot iron. Take extra care when fixing, to ensure that the fabric paint is permanent.

TIPS

o *Work from top to bottom, so that any wet areas do not smudge.*

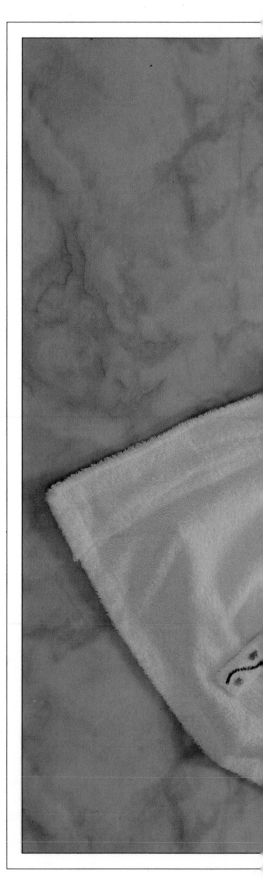

RIGHT: *Customize a bathrobe by hand-painting shapes on key areas such as the lapels, pockets and belt. The motifs used here are loosely based on Tyrolean designs.*

spatter painting

SPATTER PAINTED SHOWER CURTAIN

A spatter painted shower curtain can add a touch of creativity to an otherwise anonymous bathroom. The spray effect can be achieved in a multitude of ways, from flicking with a toothbrush to using the end of a stick. Spatter painting is ideal for beginners as it is quick and easy and fun to do. Shoe dye or car spray paints should be used for the best results, but they are not water soluble, so avoid making mistakes, as they cannot be rectified. Ordinary fabric paints will not work on plastic.

Before you start, ensure that all surrounding areas are well covered. Ideally, it is best to do this job outside. Wear old or protective clothing.

RIGHT AND ABOVE: A unique decorative touch is added to the bathroom with a see-through shower curtain, made more opaque with a one-colour spattering effect.

EQUIPMENT

plastic shower curtain
newspaper or old sheets to protect
    surroundings
shoe dye or car spray paints
clean container for mixing paints
brush or stick for flicking the paint
clean rags

METHOD

1 Make sure that the shower curtain is perfectly clean, dry and greasefree.

2 Stretch out the curtain over a flat working area. Alternatively, it could be hung from a clothesline, but this will create a streaky quality to the design as the paints will run.

3 Mix the paints if you want to create your own colours, or use them straight from the pot. Using the stick or brush, spatter and splash the dye over the shower curtain, dipping only the end of the brush or stick into the paint. Start by spattering sparsely, gradually building up the density. You can always add colour, but excessive paint will be difficult to remove.

4 If you are using more than one colour, allow the first coat to dry for a couple of hours before adding the next layer of paint. Clean the brush or stick thoroughly between colours, or you will create a muddy effect.

5 Allow the curtain to dry flat. This will take several hours. Ensure that it is perfectly dry before moving. Do not fold it on itself, or it will stick together.

6 Once dry, the paint will be permanent so there is no need for fixing.

TIPS

o *Put newspaper all the way around the edge of the shower curtain so that the design can be completed right up to the edges.*

o *Blot any thick blobs of paint with tissue paper to speed up the drying process.*

*These stunning deckchairs, painted in bold
shapes and colours, were decorated with the simple,
striking work of Henri Matisse in mind.*

OUTSIDE

The decoration of fabrics need not be limited to inside the home. A variety of different materials can be painted or printed for use in the garden or backyard, the countryside or at the beach. For home entertaining on the patio or the lawn, old outdoor furniture can be brought back to life with a little paint and imagination. Chairs which are still serviceable can easily be re-covered with painted canvas. A parasol can be made to match the chair covers, and faded and worn fabrics can be rejuvenated with fresh, bright colours. Painted scatter cushions are fun and versatile too—tough cotton fabrics are the best to use for this purpose.

Going to the beach or sitting by the pool is a lovely way to spend hot summer days. Fashion trends play a great part in swimwear and accessories. A total look can be achieved through imaginative design ideas. The motifs need not be complex in order to achieve maximum effect. The range of colour combinations is limitless, but fresh, bright colours are usually more effective when designing for outside.

Once you begin to decorate you will find the potential is unlimited. The source of inspiration can be suited to your own particular interests — windsurfing, beachcombing, shell collecting or just relaxing in the sun. Alternatively, you may prefer to keep designs simple. Good effects can be achieved with just spots and stripes. Basic sporty colours like red, white and blue are always fashionable and smart.

When decorating fabrics for outside it is particularly important to ensure that the fabric colours are fast. It would be embarrasing and disappointing if the colours in a deckchair ran when you sat down on it after a swim, or if they blurred into a muddy-looking mess on the sarong you have lovingly painted. It is, therefore, essential to read the manufacturer's instructions carefully before painting each project.

Tough, durable fabrics are best for outdoor use, but this need not prevent you from using any fabric of your choice, as long as it is appropriate to its use and suitable for the painting technique you are going to select. Nylon and synthetic fabrics are, of course, very practical for outside, but few fabric colours work well on them and they are likely to bleed. If you are going to paint on synthetics, car spray paints are ideal. The colours can be controlled by spraying through cut stencils.

Decorating fabrics for outside is always very satisfying. Unrestricted by existing decor or by space, the designs can be as bold and uninhibited as you wish. Colours and shapes can be as unconventional and fantastic as you choose because you will not have to live or sleep with them day after day. Be daring and try out unusual colour combinations and motifs—you may be delighted with the *avant garde* results.

MATISSE DECKCHAIRS

freestyle painting

Increasingly, there are more and more canvas chair designs available in the shops, but the prices are often high and the designs are not always very imaginative. Ready-made deckchairs with plain canvas seating can easily be painted in exciting colours. Alternatively, you can buy natural or coloured canvas to recover old or faded fabrics. Worn woodwork can be repainted to match, in bright, lively colours such as red, yellow or green.

When selecting canvas to work on, do not choose a colour that is too bright as the paints you work onto it will be affected by the background colour. For example, it would be very difficult to design on bright red or blue fabric with anything other than very dark paints such as black or navy blue. Therefore, light, bright colours, for example, pale yellow or peach canvas, should be used or, better still, cream or white.

For these deckchairs, natural cream canvas was selected. It is light and fresh-looking and makes an excellent base colour for fabric paints. Therefore, all the colours used have retained their clear quality.

The design inspiration was taken from the paintings of Matisse. Artists' work has been used in many different ways as an inspiration for fabric and fashion design. Deckchairs are a good-sized shape to work on when using artist's images. The basic, oblong shape of the seat allows the design to be seen clearly without fussy shaping or seaming interfering with the image. The canvas can, therefore, be worked on in a variety of different ways to create a strong effect.

Once you have decided on a theme based upon a favourite artist's work—trips to bookshops, art galleries and museums will help you gain a clearer image of what you want to create—make a number of sketches, transferring your ideas onto paper.

Once the sketches are complete, cut small oblongs of canvas. Paint your designs to scale on the miniature pieces of canvas using fabric paint. Consider the type of effect desired and the difficulty in executing the designs. Don't be overambitious in your first attempts. Decide on a design which is not too complicated—very often the simplest ideas can be the most effective.

If you are making the seating, cut the fabric considerably larger than required, leaving plenty of room for hems. The fabric will have to be stitched along both sides and several inches/centimetres must be allowed at the top and bottom for turning under and securing onto the wooden frame of the deckchair. If you are working on a chair which already has a plain canvas seating suitable for painting, the fabric can either be removed and then replaced once it has been painted, or the design can be worked while the material is in situ. If you do opt for the latter working arrangement, make sure that the wooden frame is protected from the paint with masking tape.

BELOW: The basic oblong shape of deckchairs makes them an ideal surface to work on. Ideas should be worked out in sketch form before transferring the design onto the actual fabric. As can be seen from these drawings, a large variety of themes can be tackled, although a simpler design will often be more successful than an intricate one.

EQUIPMENT

plain canvas deckchairs or canvas to
   re-cover an old deckchair
protective sheeting or paper
silk paints or fabric paints
pencil
selection of brushes
iron to fix the paints

METHOD

1 Cut the canvas fabric as advised, leaving enough material for hems.

2 Prepare the work area. A large flat surface is required which should be covered with paper or old fabric. Although it is unlikely that paint would seep through a material as thick as canvas, it is always advisable to take precautions.

3 Silk colours and fabric paints were used for these designs. They can be carefully diluted with water to make them go further, but the density of colour when dry will be paler than the wet paint. It is therefore important to see how they dry on sample pieces of fabric before embarking upon the main project.

4 Working from your sketches, draw the design onto the canvas using a pencil.

5 Apply the colour, working within the drawn pencil lines. Each colour must be completely dry before applying the next or the paints will bleed into each other. The brush must be washed between each application and carefully dried.

6 When all the colours have been applied, allow the paints to dry completely. Fix the colour by ironing both sides of the cloth with a very hot iron.

7 Sew the hems of the fabric, then secure the canvas onto the frames.

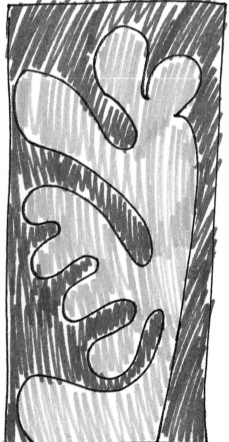

car spray paints

MATISSE BEACH MAT

The design for this beach mat was based on the work of Matisse to echo the paintings on the deckchairs. Car spray paints were used in very strong colours. Paler shades would have looked insignificant on such a dark background.

It is essential that you work in a well-ventilated area or outside, as the fumes from these paints are toxic.

EQUIPMENT

rush beach mat
protective sheeting
sheet of lining paper or wallpaper
   larger than the mat
pencil
craft knife
masking tape
car spray paints

TIPS

o *Use simple, bold shapes as the matting fibres will distort a detailed design.*

o *To prevent the colours from bleeding into each other, allow each one to dry before applying the next colour.*

RIGHT: Beach mats can usually only be bought in natural colours. By adding a colourful sprayed design a really original effect can be achieved.

METHOD

1 Prepare the work area. All surrounding surfaces must be well-covered. No matter how careful you are, there will be considerable amounts of paint sprayed over the working area.

2 Prepare a stencil the same size as the beach mat. Lining paper or wallpaper is ideal. Draw the shapes you want to colour on it, then cut them out of the paper using a sharp knife. Place the stencil over the mat and tape it into place using masking tape.

3 Spray the required colours through the holes into the stencil working from directly above. These paints spray outwards over a large area, so if the hole you are spraying is close to another one, cover the other open areas with paper to prevent the spray from falling where the colour is not required. Some respraying may be necessary to ensure a good, even coverage of colour.

4 Allow the mat to dry in a well-ventilated area. This should only take half an hour, but leave it overnight until the fumes disappear.

5 There is no need to fix these paints. Your mat is now ready to roll up and take to the water's edge.

spatter painting

JACKSON POLLOCK CHAIR

The decoration for this chair was based on the lively, splashed paintings of Jackson Pollock. Although a lot of his work used black and grey, a palette of fresh spring colours was selected for a bright, sunny effect. The splashed, dripped and drawn marks made on the canvas create an appealing effect. This chair was made in natural wood, but others can be painted to co-ordinate with the canvas decoration.

EQUIPMENT
plain canvas deckchair or canvas to recover an old deckchair
sheeting or paper to protect work surface and surrounding areas
masking tape
silk paints and/or fabric paints
containers for mixing and diluting colours
large household brush
iron to fix the paints

METHOD

1 A large table or floor space is needed when using this painting technique. If possible, the spraying should be done outside where stray splatterings of paint will not be a problem. If you are working indoors, all surfaces in the room must be covered with protective fabric sheeting or newspaper.

2 Stretch out the canvas and secure it in place with tape at each corner.

3 Silk paints and fabric paints were used for this chair. Make sure that you have plenty of paint, as the splash effect can use up a lot of colour very quickly! Silk paints are available in an exciting range of colours and do not usually need mixing. However, they can be diluted with a little water to make the colours less intense and cover a greater area. Pour the paints into clean containers to work from.

4 The splash effect is achieved by dipping a large household brush brush into the paint. Stand over the fabric and jerk the wrist downwards.

A stronger effect can be achieved by moving the elbow. Apply the colours in sequence, starting with the yellow and orange and allow them to dry before applying the next colour. The darkest colour—blue—should be applied last. The drying time varies with the temperature you are working in, although it can be speeded up by using a hairdryer. If all the colours are applied at once, the splashes will overlap and merge together creating a muddy effect.

5 Add a few blobs of paint in yellow, orange and blue. Drag the end of the brush over them across the canvas to give broken marks. If so desired, more colours can be added to give more density to the design.

6 Allow the painted fabric to dry completely. Fix the colour by ironing both sides of the cloth with a very hot iron.

7 Sew the hems of the fabric, then secure it to the chair frame.

TIPS
o *Both silk paints and fabric paints were used for the decoration of this chair. They cannot be blended together, so it is very important to let each colour dry before applying the next one. Do not over-dilute the silk paints.*

RIGHT: This deck chair was simply decorated with a mixture of fresh colours splashed onto the canvas fabric.

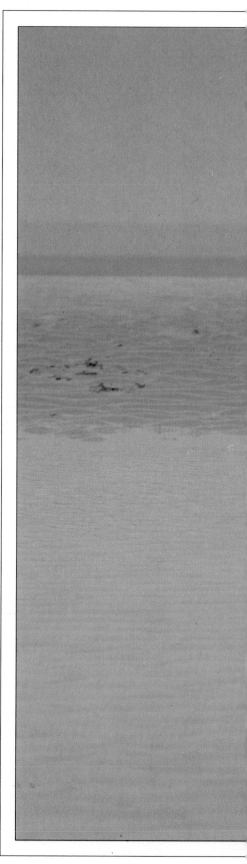

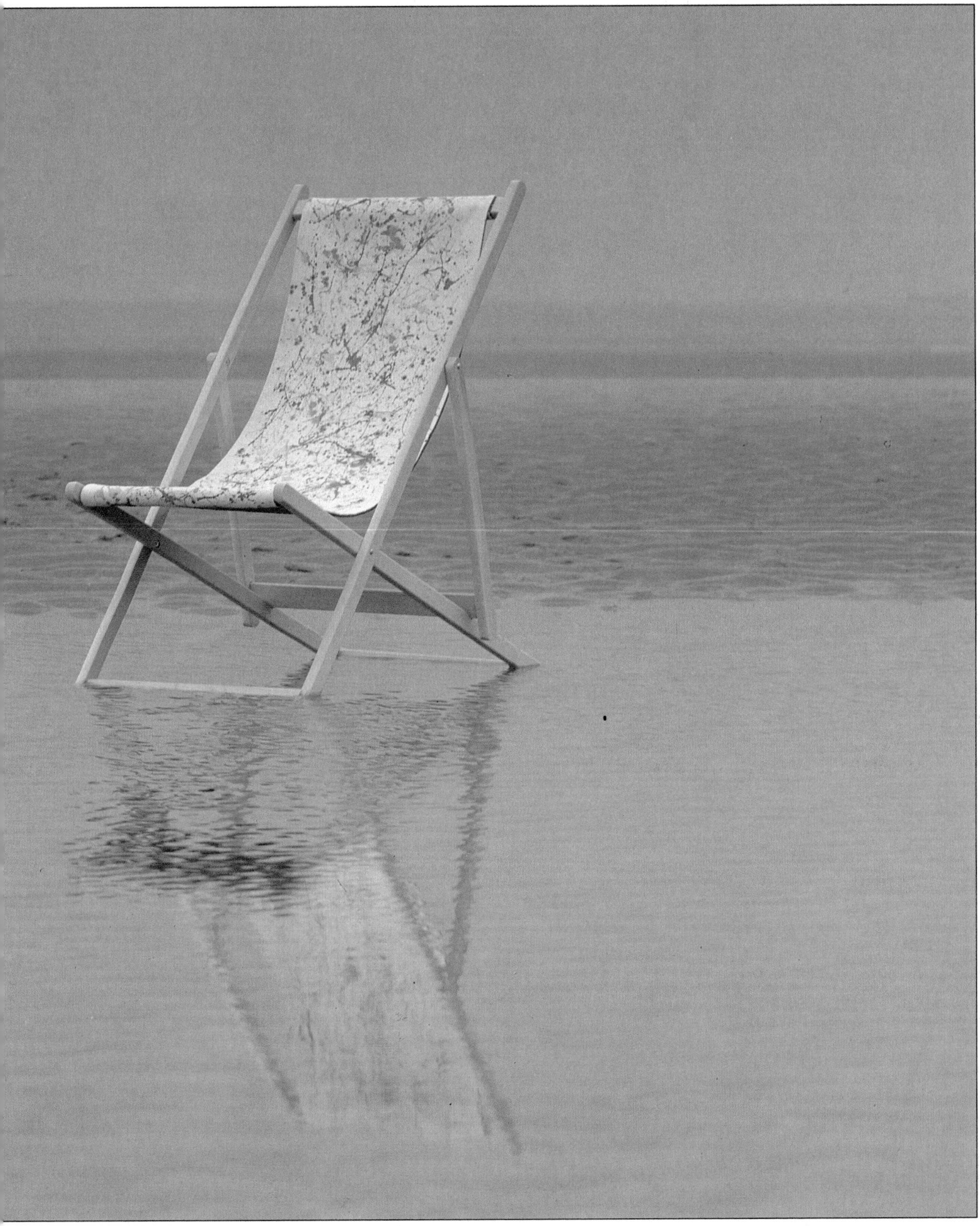

The sketches in the top row are based on
Jackson Pollock's work, studying how best his
exciting splashed work can be adapted to the
canvas of the deckchairs. Other artists' work
has been looked at in the sketches below,
simplifying and stylizing the shapes and
colours.

BEACH SHOES

Plain beach shoes have been splashed with shoe dye to create a bright, original effect. Several colours can be used for this type of painting, but each colour must be allowed to dry completely before adding another. This may take several hours, so allow lots of time for this project if you are planning to use more than one colour.

EQUIPMENT

fabric beach shoes
lots of newspaper
paint brushes
shoe dye
large container for paint

METHOD

1 Cover your work area with newspaper. If possible, work outside to prevent any splashes of paint from falling onto surfaces other than those intended.

2 Fill each shoe with thick tissue or newspaper to prevent the inside of the shoe from being painted. This will also give you something to hold when you are painting, as you will need to rotate the shoe as you work.

3 It is a good idea to try out some preliminary experiments before painting the shoes to ascertain the type of splash marks you require. You will be surprised at the variety of effects which can be achieved by varying the movement of the arm and wrist. The size of the brush used will also determine the quantity of colour applied to the fabric. The larger the brush, the bigger the splash effects.

4 Pour the shoe dye into a container large enough to dip your brush into. Old foil containers from pre-packed foods are ideal. Remember that the container will almost certainly be stained and spoiled by the dye, so don't use anything which is not disposable.

5 Place the shoes on the covered work area and splash the paint onto them, using flicking motions. Remember to cover the sides of the shoes as well as the top. When complete, leave the shoes to dry. Once dry, other colours may be used, if desired. On a small area such as this, one colour is often more effective than several, which, from a distance may give the impression of merging into each other.

6 Shoe dye does not require fixing and, once dry, will be permanent.

BELOW: Before deciding upon the colours and quality of splashes to be used for the beach shoes (shown overleaf), shoe shapes were cut out of paper and then splashed with paint, creating varied effects.

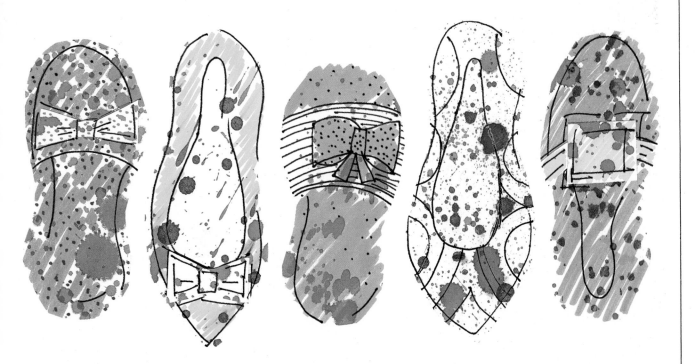

spatter painting

BEACH TOWEL

This towel was made from a length of terrycloth towelling which was simply hemmed at the top and the bottom. However, if you prefer to work on a ready-made towel, this will be just as effective, as long as you make sure that it is 100% cotton.

Blue and red were selected for a clean, fresh effect and to co-ordinate with the beach shoes.

Consideration must be given to the work area when preparing to splash a large towel. Working outside is always the best solution, to avoid splashing furniture, walls or carpets. If this is not possible, carefully cover all areas of the room with newspaper or cotton sheeting.

EQUIPMENT

towel or towelling fabric
protective sheeting or newspaper
fabric paints
large containers
selection of household brushes
clean cloth for ironing
iron to fix the paints

LEFT: Fashion can be fun on the beach. Beach shoes or towels can be decorated to co-ordinate with your swimsuit or bikini. These simple white accessories have been transformed by simply splattering them with fabric paint.

METHOD

1 Prepare your work area, ensuring that all surrounding areas are well protected.

2 Pour the paints into clean containers, allowing for the different brush sizes you may be using for splashing.

3 Decide on the type of splash effect you wish to achieve on the towel. Being a large piece of fabric, considerable freedom can be exercised in creating different markings.

4 Stretch the towel over the working area and splash it with the first colour—in this case, blue. Allow the paint to dry. The second colour, red, is then applied, evenly distributing the marks over the towel. Allow the paint to dry.

5 Fix the fabric paints by ironing evenly across the back and the front of the towel with a hot iron. You may want to place a cloth between the towel and the ironing board to protect the surface of the ironing board.

RAINBOW SARONG

The versatility of a silk sarong is limitless. It can be wrapped, draped, tied or knotted in an endless variety of different ways. The decoration on this sarong illustrates how a simple design and painting technique, executed in a limited colour range, can produce lovely results.

EQUIPMENT

length of fine silk
cotton sheeting to protect the work
    surface
masking tape
silk paints
clean containers for the paints
pieces of natural sponge—one for
    each colour
clean cloth for ironing
iron to fix the paints

METHOD

1 Cover the work area with cotton sheeting. Because the fabric used is very thin, a lot of paint will pass through onto the work surface, so a good covering is needed. Make sure that all your utensils are near at hand.

2 Lay the silk on the backing cloth and secure it down with masking tape.

3 Prepare your paints by putting them into clean containers which are large enough for you to dip the corner of the sponge into. Do not overload the sponge with paint.

4 A simple stripe is created by sponging directly onto the silk, moving the sponge from one side of the fabric to the other. The width of the stripe is up to you. Because the silk is so fine, the paint will bleed beautifully into the fabric.

LEFT: An attractive accessory for the beach is a sarong—especially if it is silk. It can be decorated in a number of different ways. Here simple sponged stripes and a more complicated screen printing technique have been used.

5 Continue working the colours in turn, using a clean sponge for each colour. Because the stripes on the sarong are positioned quite far apart, it is not necessary to wait for each colour to dry.

6 Once you are happy with your design, allow the sarong to dry completely. It should be left to dry on the work surface, away from direct heat or sunlight.

7 Fix the colours by ironing the silk on a medium hot iron. Take care not to scorch the fabric.

8 Hem the ends of the silk and your sarong is complete.

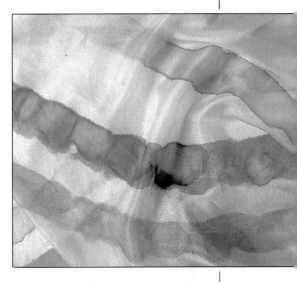

ABOVE: This detail shows how the silk paints have bled freely into the delicate silk, forming loose, unstructured patterns.

silk screen printing

MIGRATING BIRDS SARONG

The use of screen printing has revolutionized the fabric industry. The styles and effects that can be achieved are almost limitless and most of the fabrics we see in the shops today are screen printed. Of course, screen printing at home must be tackled in a more modest way than commercial work, where the elaborate equipment used would be prohibitively expensive—and large—for the amateur fabric painter to consider. However, the basic method of screen printing is really very simple (see page 95) and gives the textile printer great scope.

EQUIPMENT

length of fine silk
protective blanket and fabric sheeting
    for the work surface
paper
craft knife
clean containers to mix the paints
fabric printing colours
masking tape
screen printing frame and squeegee
iron to fix the paint

METHOD

1 Prepare your print table. A dining room table or kitchen table can be used if it is well protected. Cover the surface with a blanket taking care to avoid seams or joins which will affect the even printing surface. Cover the blanket with a sheet or length of cotton. Secure these two layers firmly to the print table.

2 Work out your design on paper. The inspiration for this pattern was taken from a flock of migrating birds in autumn.

3 Once you are happy with your design, carefully cut the design out of paper using a craft knife.

4 Prepare your paints in clean containers.

5 For a perfectly smooth result, iron the fabric on the work surface, removing all creases, then secure it in place with masking tape.

6 Place the paper stencil on the fabric. The screen is then placed face down on it. Pour the fabric colour into the well at one end of the screen, then draw the colour firmly across the screen using the squeegee. To ensure that the print is dark enough, pull the squeegee back across the screen.

7 Continue to print the pattern randomly over the fabric. If the screen is placed over or near a wet print, it is advisable to cover the wet image with newsprint to prevent a shadow from being picked up on the printing screen.

8 Once you are satisfied with the fabric, allow it to dry leaving it in place on the print table. The fabric should not be subjected to direct heat or sunlight.

9 Fix the colours by carefully ironing the reverse side of the fabric, taking care not to scorch the material.

TIPS

o *When using a paper stencil, the screen must be washed as soon as you have finished printing to prevent blocking of the screen mesh. Consequently, the paper stencil will be lost. More permanent methods can be used—art shops sell stencils which allow the screen to be washed after printing and the stencil can be re-used.*

o *When printing several colours, each colour will require a separate paper stencil.*

ABOVE: When screen printing a delicate material like this silk, two pulls of the squeegee are sufficient for a clear print. However, a heavier material will need three, four or even five pulls of colour. Sample pieces of fabric should always be prepared before starting the main project.

SUMMER PICNIC

There are many occasions when a picnic hamper will prove invaluable, especially during the summer months. This wicker hamper (shown overleaf) was bought from an antique shop and lined with a hand-printed, tough, heavyweight cotton canvas. The tablecloth and hats were made as practical and attractive accessories to the hamper.

The design of simple spots was chosen as a fresh, bright contrast to rather heavy wicker exterior of the hamper. Decorating the fabric is, of course, a matter of taste. Any style of design could have been used, for instance summer landscapes or flowers. Alternatively, forks and spoons dipped in fabric colour could be pressed onto the fabric to give interesting effects. Apples cut in half also give good clear prints. For this fabric design, old wine corks were used for printing.

Only the very top of the cork should be immersed in dye for printing. Overloading the cork with paint may cause it to drip onto the fabric. It will also hide the lovely textured quality of the cork, leaving a thick, uninteresting layer of paint on the material.

ABOVE: These samplers have been decorated using a combination of potato printing, brush stokes and a fork dipped in dye.

EQUIPMENT

heavyweight cotton canvas
wicker picnic hamper
hat
newsprint
protective fabric or newsprint
fabric paints
clean containers
masking tape
corks for printing
iron to fix the paints
wadding (batting)

METHOD

1 Work out how much fabric will be needed for lining the picnic basket by laying newsprint over the lid and the interior. Cut paper patterns, allowing for seams and folds. Lay the paper patterns over the canvas material which you are going to use for printing, and cut out the required pieces. With the remaining material, cut the fabric for the tablecloth.

2 Prepare your work surface by covering it with old fabric or newsprint. As the cotton canvas is quite thick, little or no dye colour will penetrate through the cloth onto the work surface. However, it is always advisable to cover the work surface.

3 Experiment with sample pieces of fabric, working out the pattern and the colours you are going to use. In this case, four colours were selected to complement each other and to show up clearly on the pale cream canvas background.

4 Prepare your fabric paints in clean containers, mixing colours and shades, as necessary.

5 Lay the fabric pieces on the prepared work area. Tape them down onto the work surface using masking tape to keep them in place while working.

6 Dip the cork into the first printing colour, then press it down firmly onto the fabric. Repeat the process, keeping the cork well covered in dye to give a good, solid spot. If any imperfections occur, this will add to the effect and give textural interest to the design. Work the spots regularly across all the fabric pieces using the first colour. Allow space for the spots in different colours.

7 There is no need to allow the first colour to dry, as the application of the second colour will not affect the first one. Continue to print the third and then the the fourth colours. Allow the colours to dry.

8 Stand back from the fabric and ensure that each piece has an even distribution of colour. If not, add extra prints where necessary. Allow the paints to dry.

9 To fix the colour, iron the fabric on the back and the front with a hot iron, taking care not to scorch the fabric.

10 Place a piece of wadding (batting) on the back of each fabric piece and secure it to the fabric with glue or by stitching. Place the pieces in position in the hamper and fasten in place with glue or by stitching. Hem the edges of the tablecloth.

TIPS

o *It can be fun thinking of ways of co-ordinating fabrics. In this case, a band was made for the straw hat to match the picnic basket and tablecloth. A small strip of fabric left over from the hamper pieces was printed with spots in the same colours. The edges of the fabric were then hemmed and a flat bow was made as a feature for the hat.*

TIPS

o When selecting a picnic hamper, do not choose one with lots of compartments as this will make it difficult to line the hamper with fabric.

o A hard-wearing cotton canvas is ideal for this project. Do not select a delicate fabric which will not stand up to the wear and tear it will be subjected to.

BELOW: The hard-wearing canvas used for these picnic accessories has been printed with a cork dipped in fabric paints. The colours for the design were carefully blended for a colourful, but sophisticated effect.

plastic paints

PVC Picnic Cloth

The decoration of fabrics need not be applied only to natural fabrics. There are now a wide selection of fabric paints available which have been specially manufactured for use on man-made materials.

Here, a bright yellow plastic cloth has been decorated with stripes and checks randomly scattered over its surface, giving a lively, exciting result. These paints are not affected by the background colour, so a brilliant yellow was selected to work on. However, as they are not absorbed into the fabric, they should not be used over a large area or too thickly, as the surface will become bumpy, and the paint may peel off the fabric.

A ready-made tablecloth can be decorated or, alternatively, the PVC fabric can be purchased by the metre/yard. The fabric is durable and hard-wearing and can easily be wiped clean.

You can use an abstract pattern, or the cloth can be decorated for special occasions, such as children's birthdays. Names or pictorial motifs can be drawn on the fabric. These paints are very quick and easy to use and will give instant, fun results.

EQUIPMENT

length of plastic or plastic tablecloth
protective newspaper or old cloth
masking tape
plastic-finish paints

TIPS

o *Should the paints be accidentally squeezed onto something they can be removed — with difficulty — with white spirit (turpentine) and steel wool.*

METHOD

1 Protect your working area with newspaper or an old cloth. Plastic finish paints are very difficult to remove if they are accidentally squeezed onto something.

2 Stretch out the fabric over the working area, fastening it down at the edges so that it does not slip. You may want to mark your design on it with a soft pencil as a guideline.

3 These types of paints are packed in plastic containers with a nozzle. The container is simply pressed and the colour comes out of the nozzle to form lines of colour. Do not use the paints too thickly, or over too large an area.

4 Leave the paint to dry overnight. These paints take a long time to dry, so make sure that the design is not still tacky before using it, or before folding up the cloth.

RIGHT AND ABOVE: Plastic coated fabric is ideal for a children's tablecloth. This brightly-coloured cloth has been decorated with plastic paints, which can also be wiped clean.

SPOTTED UMBRELLA

Simple designs such as spots and stripes can be used to achieve lively, eye-catching effects.

There are a number of techniques which can be used to create spotted patterns. For instance, spots can be printed using a variety of round objects which are dipped in dye and then pressed onto the surface of the fabric. Corks or carrot tops will all give a round print. The size of the circle will, of course, depend upon the size of the object used.

The spots on this umbrella were made by using a stencil cut out of a very large piece of cardboard, and car spray paints. Ordinary fabric paints would have bled into the synthetic material. However, if you are working on a cotton umbrella, fabric paints can be used.

If you are working on synthetic material using car spray paints, it is important to remember that the fumes of these paints are poisonous and should not be breathed in. The work should, preferably, be done outside. The umbrella should also be allowed to dry in a well-ventilated area as the paints remain noxious until they are absolutely dry.

ABOVE: Car spray paints can be used to create exciting designs on synthetic umbrellas. A simple, spotted pattern in bright colours was selected for this umbrella.

EQUIPMENT

synthetic umbrella
protective sheeting or newspaper
thick cardboard for the stencil
car spray paint

METHOD

1 Prepare your work area, protecting all nearby surfaces, as car spray paints cannot be removed from furnishing fabrics. It is important that you work in a very well-ventilated area, preferably outside.

2 Experiment with the shapes and colours that you are planning to use before embarking on the main project.

3 Cut out the stencil. It is vital that you cut it out of a very large piece of cardboard to protect the rest of the umbrella from stray paint.

4 Open the umbrella out on the work surface. Lay the stencil in position and spray into the circular shape for a few seconds. Do not spray for too long, as the paint will run if the area is too thickly coated. Remove the stencil.

5 Repeat this process using the first colour all around the umbrella, spacing the circle shapes evenly over its surface. Allow the paint to dry completely.

6 Wipe the stencil clean. Repeat the process with the second colour and allow the shapes to dry.

7 There is no need for fixing, as these colours are permanent once they have dried.

RIGHT AND BELOW Lots of exciting, original design ideas can be used to transform a plain parasol.

SORBET PICNIC CLOTH

A tablecloth decorated in pleasing colours can make a marvellous accessory for your picnic—it will even make the food seem more attractive and appealing.

This tablecloth has been decorated with clear, summery colours, conjuring up the flavours of summer foods—fresh fruits, summer wines and cool, refreshing desserts. A great deal of time was spent choosing clear, warm colours which worked well together to capture a summery feeling. The colours have been sponged onto the fabric, laying colours over each other to blend, creating new shades.

Before you start, preliminary samplers should be made to assess the amount of bleed on the fabric and to see how your selected colours work together. The colours on the cloth have been watered down to give pale tones and soft effects. This also encouraged the paints to bleed freely into each other.

EQUIPMENT

cotton tablecloth or fabric
fabric sheeting or newsprint to
    protect your work surface
silk paints
pieces of natural sponge—one for
    each colour
clean containers for mixing the
    paints
clean cloth for ironing
iron to fix the paints

TIPS

o *To create a more unusual pattern, the design for the tablecloth was worked from the outer edge into the middle. The intensity of the colour on the outer frame gradually becomes softer, with the areas of sponging more spaced out towards the middle of the cloth.*

o *It is always a good idea, when purchasing fabric for printing, to buy a little extra for trial samples.*

o *To complete the picnic accessories, matching napkins can be made. Keep the tablecloth close by, so that the pattern and the colours are complementary.*

METHOD

1 Prepare your work area, covering it with fabric sheeting or newsprint. A good-sized surface will be needed for working on the tablecloth.

2 Mix the silk paints in clean containers. For softer effects, water can be added.

3 Dip the sponge into the palest colour, taking care not to overload it with paint. In this case, the palest colour is yellow. Sponge the paint evenly onto the cloth over the square area of the pattern.

4 Apply the second colour. In this case, it should be pink. The yellow and the pink will blend beautifully into each other, creating soft peach and orangey colours.

5 Allow the paler colours to dry before adding the darker shades. If the green is allowed to bleed into the other colours, a muddy and dull effect will result.

6 Allow the colours to dry completely. Assess your finished work. If you wish, additional sponging can be added.

7 When the cloth is completely dry, fix the paints by ironing both the back and the front of the fabric with a hot iron.

RIGHT Watered-down silk paints have been sponged onto cotton fabric to create the muted, but clear, fresh colours of this picnic cloth. The paints were allowed to bleed into each other, forming lovely new shades of colour.

STAIN REMOVAL

Certain materials, particularly those which have been painted or dyed, can be damaged by proprietary cleaners, which may also 'lift' the paint out of the fabric. It is, therefore, essential to test a small part of the material with the cleaning agent first. Always treat fabric with great care. Do not rub delicate fabrics when removing stains; it will damage the fibres. Methylated spirit and white spirit should not be used as cleaning agents on man-made fabrics.

When sponging material to remove a stain, sponge from the edges of the stain, working inwards. This will prevent a water mark from developing. All spillages should be dealt with as soon as they occur so that the stain does not have a chance to penetrate and settle into the fabric fibres.

ANIMAL STAINS
Most types of animal stains (vomit, urine etc.) can be treated by soaking the fabric overnight in a solution of warm water and biological soap powder. The item should then be washed in a biological powder.

BLOOD
Sponge the stain with cold water; hot water will make the stain permanent. Soak the fabric overnight in tepid soapy water.

CHEWING GUM
Place the fabric in the freezer. Once frozen, the chewing gum will crack and can be peeled off the material. Any remnants can be removed with white spirit.

CHOCOLATE
Soak the fabric overnight in a solution of biological washing powder, then wash the fabric as usual, using a biological washing powder.

COFFEE
Soak the fabric overnight in a solution of biological washing powder, then wash the fabric as usual, using a biological washing powder.

EGG
Sponge the stain with a solution of cold, salty water. Do not use hot water because it will set the stain.

FRUIT
If possible, stretch the material over a container and pour boiling water from a kettle over the stain. Take great care that the steam from the kettle does not scald your arms. Obviously, this method is not suitable for delicate fabrics which can be sponged with liquid detergent.

GLUE
Place a clean piece of cotton wool over the stain. Soak another piece of cotton wool with non-oily nail varnish remover and dab the other side of the stain. Nail varnish remover is not suitable for man-made materials.

GRASS
Sponge the stain with a clean rag soaked in methylated spirit, then wash the fabric with a biological powder.

GREASE
Eucalyptus oil will remove oily, greasy stains without leaving a water mark. If you do not have eucalyptus oil at home, sponge the stain with undiluted liquid detergent and then wash the fabric with a biological washing powder.

MAKE-UP
Sponge the stain with undiluted liquid detergent. Leave the detergent to penetrate the fabric for five minutes, then rinse well with cold water. For man-made fabrics, the detergent should be diluted. Wash the fabric as usual with a biological washing powder.

MILD SCORCH MARKS
Unfortunately, heavy scorch marks cannot be treated because the fabric has been permanently damaged. Mild scorch marks can be minimized by sponging the fabric immediately with a solution of cold water and sugar.

NAIL VARNISH
Place a clean pice of cotton wool over the stain. Soak another piece of cotton wool with non-oily nail varnish remover and dab the other side of the stain. Take great care to work inwards from the edges of the stain so that you do not spread the mark over the fabric.

WINE
Both red and white wine stains can be removed by smearing a solution of lemon juice and salt over the stain, rinsing the material, and then washing it in a biological soap powder. Red wine stains can be treated by sponging them with a generous quantity of white wine. Alternatively, a red wine stain can be treated by pouring salt over it. This will soak up the wine.

USEFUL ADDRESSES

Nearly all the fabrics, paints and dyes and accessories mentioned in this book can be bought in local artist's suppliers, fabric shops and DIY stores. Listed below are main retail outlets, many of whom offer a mail order service, and distributors who can put you in touch with your nearest retail outlets.

FABRIC SUPPLIERS

G.P. & J. Baker Limited,
18 Berners Street,
London W1P 4UA.

Baumann Fabrics Limited,
41-42 Berners Street,
London W1.

Brooke Fairbairn & Co.,
The Railway Station,
Newmarket,
Suffolk CB8 9BA.

Busby & Busby Limited,
57 Salisbury Street,
Blandford Forum,
Dorset DT11 7PY.

Designer's Guild,
271 Kings Road,
London SW3.

Fox & Floor,
142 Royal College Street,
London NW1 07A.

John Lewis,
Oxford Street,
London W1.

Liberty,
Regents Street,
London W1.

Hill & Knowles Limited,
133 Kew Road,
Richmond,
Surrey TW9 2PN.

MacCulloch & Wallis Limited,
25-26 Dering Street,
London W1R 0BH.

Marvic Textiles,
12-14 Mortimer Street,
London W1N 7RD.

Ian Mankin,
109 Regents Park Road,
London NW1.

Osborne & Little,
304 King's Road,
London SW3.

Russell & Chapple,
33 Monmouth Street,
London WC2.

Ian Sanderson (Textiles) Limited,
70 Cleveland Street,
London W1P 3DD.

Timney Fowler,
388 Kings Road,
London SW3.

George Weill,
Riding House Street,
London W1.

ARTIST'S SUPPLIERS

Cowling and Wilcox,
26-28 Broadwick Street,
London W1.

Bolloms,
107-115 Long Acre,
London WC2

Dylon International Limited,
Worsley Bridge Road,
Lower Sydenham,
London SE26.

Frisk Products,
7-11 Franthorne Way,
Randlesdown Road,
London SE6 3BT.

H.W. Peel & Co.,
Norwester House,
Fairway Drive,
Greenford,
Middlesex UB6 8PW.

Plotons,
273 Archway Road,
London N6.

Carolyn Warrender,
91-93 Lower Sloane Street,
London SW1.

G.H. Smith & Partners,
Berechurch Road,
Colchester,
Essex CO2 7QF.

Windsor and Newton,
51 Rathbone Place,
London W1.

PUBLISHER'S CREDITS

The publishers would like to express their grateful thanks to the following artists, shops and galleries for their help and advice in the compilation of this book. Their contributions are listed below:

Pages 8/9: Wall hanging by Nicola Henley. Her work is available at The Contemporary Textile Gallery, 10 Golden Square, London W1.
Page 32: Picture by Jacqueline Guille. Her work is available at The Contemporary Textile Gallery.
Pages 34/35: Vase from Timney Fowler, 388 Kings Road, London SW3. Picture by Michael B. White.
Flooring by Nairn, Forbo-Nairn Information Service, Old Loom House, Back Church Lane, London E1 1LS.
Page 39: Chair and pot from L.M. Kingcome Limited.
Page 41: Chair by Jennie Moncur; rug by Helen Yardley. Their work is available at The Contemporary Textile Gallery.
Page 42: Chair by Carmels and Son.
Pages 44/45: Chair by Ray McNeil. Screen by Ray McNeil and Ian Wright. Their workshop is at 124 Curtain Road, London EC1.
Pages 54/55: Cushions by Ann Chiswell, Ann Chiswell Designs, 34 Queens Drive, London W3.
Pages 57-59: Pictures by Susan Kennewell, The Contemporary Textile Gallery.
Page 61: Picture by Claudine Dungen, The Contemporary Textile Gallery.
Page 64: Hanging by Steven Pettengell, The Contemporary Textile Gallery.
Page 72: Floor rug by Jona Carlyn. The Contemporary Textile Gallery.
Pages 78/79: Vase and cups and saucers from Timney Fowler.
Pages 82/83: Napkins by Jill Dickinson.
Brass candlesticks from L.M. Kingcome.
Pages 84/85: Napkins by Dylon.
Page 86: Tablecloth by Jill Dickinson.
Pages 88/89: Fabric from Timney Fowler.
Page 99: Silk painted by Ann Chiswell.
Page 105: Bedspread by Dylon.
Pages 112/113: Cot and chest by Ray McNeil, Crucial Gallery, 204 Kensington Park Road, London W11.
Page 124: Towel rail from Bisque, 244 Belsize Road, London NW6.
Pages 125 and 127: Flooring by Nairn.

The publishers are grateful to Anna Selby and Laurence Isaacson who allowed their houses to be photographed, and to Humpherson's Bathrooms and Kitchens in Chiswick, London W4, who allowed us to photograph their bathrooms.

Fabric samples on pages 20, 21 and 23 by Kate Long.

INDEX

Page numbers in *italics* refer to illustrations.

ACKNOWLEDGEMENTS

The publisher thanks the following photographers and organizations for their kind permission to reproduce the photographs in this book:

Pins & Needles magazine: pages 26/27
Ronald Sheridan (Ancient Art & Architecture Collection): page 14
The Tate Gallery: pages 11, 12 and 16
Victoria and Albert Musem: pages 15, 18 and 19

All other photographs were taken especially for Salamander Books Limited by John Cook.